MW00477419

HEMINGWAY'S PASSIONS

HEMINGWAY'S PASSIONS
His Women, His Wars, and His Writing

NANCY W. SINDELAR

LYONS
PRESS

Essex, Connecticut

An imprint of The Globe Pequot Publishing Group, Inc.
64 South Main Street
Essex, CT 06426
www.globepequot.com

Distributed by NATIONAL BOOK NETWORK

British Library Cataloguing in Publication Information available

Library of Congress Cataloging-in-Publication Data
Names: Sindelar, Nancy W., 1944– author.
Title: Hemingway's passions : his women, his wars, and his writing / Nancy W. Sindelar.
Description: Essex, Connecticut : Lyons Press, [2024] | Includes bibliographical references.
Identifiers: LCCN 2024012897 (print) | LCCN 2024012898 (ebook) | ISBN 9781493084685
    (cloth) | ISBN 9781493084692 (epub)
Subjects: LCSH: Hemingway, Ernest, 1899-1961—Relations with women. | Hemingway, Ernest,
    1899-1961—Criticism and interpretation. | American literature—20th century—History and
    criticism.
Classification: LCC PS3515.E37 Z8294 2024 (print) | LCC PS3515.E37 (ebook) | DDC
    813/.52 [B]—dc23/eng/20240709
LC record available at https://lccn.loc.gov/2024012897
LC ebook record available at https://lccn.loc.gov/2024012898

♾™ The paper used in this publication meets the minimum requirements of American National
Standard for Information Sciences—Permanence of Paper for Printed Library Materials, ANSI/
NISO Z39.48-1992.

"No matter how being in love comes out,
it's sure worth it all while it's going on."[1]

Contents

Author's Note

The Use of Letters

ERNEST HEMINGWAY AND HIS FRIENDS, FAMILY, WIVES, AND LOVERS were prodigious letter writers. While they never intended for their correspondence to be published, their letters shed invaluable light on the thoughts and emotions that influenced their relationships. Though Ernest said he wrote letters because "it's fun to get letters back," he left clear directives to his heirs that his correspondence should never be published (see epilogue).[1] However, twenty years after his death, his fourth wife and literary executor, Mary Welsh Hemingway, authorized the 1981 publication of *Ernest Hemingway: Selected Letters: 1917–1961*, edited by Carlos Baker, and in 2011 his son, Patrick, and the Hemingway Foundation gave permission for the extensive Hemingway Letters Project conducted by Sandra Spanier and Pennsylvania State University.

The quotations from letters in *Hemingway's Passions* are used to provide insight and enrich the reader's understanding of the relationships that were so important to the development of Ernest's character, life experiences, and writing. Because Ernest distinguished between letter writing and "writing that counts," he was meticulous in crafting his written work intended for publication but didn't worry that his personal letters contained misspelled words, slang, and grammatical errors. Thus, Ernest's letters, as well as those he received, are reproduced here as they were written and without corrections.

Because Ernest became famous at the early age of twenty-six, many recipients saved his letters. Others, because of the emotional content of the correspondence, destroyed them. Domenico Caracciolo, the Italian officer Agnes von Kurowsky never married, demanded that she burn the letters she received from Ernest. Hadley Richardson, Ernest's first wife, destroyed his early love letters at the time of their divorce. Pauline Pfeiffer, Ernest's second wife, didn't want her correspondence with her famous husband to be immortalized and left instructions that it be burned at the time of her death. All the correspondence did not survive, yet the extant letters serve to paint an informed picture of the personal ambition, heartbreak, and literary triumphs and trials of the iconic American writer.

Foreword

WHEN I WAS ASKED TO WRITE THE FOREWORD FOR *HEMINGWAY'S PAS-sions*, I approached the manuscript with discernment. Covering Ernest Hemingway's life truly requires a particular level of skill and dedication. If not approached and executed properly, the writing would not appropriately depict one of the most profound writers in history. However, in reading these pages, I became captivated and wholeheartedly agreed to endorse the book. *Hemingway's Passions* is a remarkable read. I offer that not just because I am his granddaughter, but because it gives Hemingway enthusiasts a profound insight into how Ernest's brain worked and how he told his stories.

This book delivers the experience of Hemingway's life through his greatest loves. Nancy Sindelar delves into Ernest's true passions—his women, his wars, and his writing—and how they shaped every choice he made. In *Hemingway's Passions*, you embark on a journey into the heart of a man whose life was as compelling as the stories he penned. This book is not merely a biography but an exploration of a soul—my grandfather's soul—torn between the twin poles of love and death, always writing, always living with unparalleled intensity.

Hemingway had an innate passion for *passion*, a concept that is deeply fascinating to me. He was obsessed with love, and equally in love with the danger of facing death. Love and war were unequivocally linked to his perspective, philosophy, and actions.

"*Grace under pressure*" is a phrase that encapsulates his quest to live more vividly, see more keenly, and feel more deeply than any before him. Whether on the bloody frontlines as a journalist or an ambulance driver, or in the savage beauty of the African savannah as a hunter, for Ernest, to face death was to face himself.

Upon his returning to the mundaneness of everyday life, the *regular* world, the only way to reignite that kind of passion was through the electrifying lure of love. The saying about a thin line between love and hatred plays out in this book. After experiencing a love lost or the tragedies of war, only that deep thirst for life would cause someone to courageously continue walking toward the danger. But is facing true love all that different from facing the fears of death? Ernest was constantly excavating these questions, and this brave book leans into those conversations, illuminating such meaningful introspections.

While reading this book, I contemplated my grandfather's life and was struck with the parallels between his battles and his romances, each feeding into the other, a perpetual cycle of inspiration that fueled his quest for that "one true sentence." Ernest Hemingway courted danger with the zeal of a lover, seeking in its embrace a truth about himself and the world around him.

Reflecting on the bittersweet end of his marriage to Hadley, my grandmother, Ernest wrote a poignant expression of love that transcends the pages of *A Moveable Feast*:

> When I saw my wife again standing by the tracks as the train came in by the piled logs at the station, I wished I had died before I ever loved anyone but her. She was smiling, the sun on her lovely face tanned by the snow and sun, beautifully built, her hair red gold in the sun, grown out all winter awkwardly and beautifully.

Respectfully, these words weigh even more heavily coming from my direct lineage. I am moved to tears when I read that passage, because Ernest was writing about the profound love he felt for Hadley. Despite their divorce, that love would last his lifetime.

Written toward the twilight of his life, after he was remarried and in the midst of a struggle with mental health and writing, these words reveal a man for whom love was not just a theme but a lifeline. Even as he navigated the complexities of fame, mental health struggles, and the ceaseless pursuit of artistic perfection, the memory of Hadley remained a touchstone of genuine affection and regret. (Also, as an aside, my middle name is Hadley, so I will always cherish that part of his memoir.)

Ernest made choices to love other women; at a deep level, those choices were a part of his art and his ability to write from a place of rare simplicity and raw emotion. His stories and novels were influenced by his life experiences with each of the women he loved: Agnes, Hadley, Pauline, Martha, and Mary . . . and those were just his *wives*. The women who were the center of his passionate love affairs (often) became his wives, and the other women with whom he had infatuations became further muses, giving him energy and poignant words to build his craft.

Those feelings of passion were matched only by the dangers of war or by looking into the face of a lion who would sooner kill him than walk away from the muzzle of his gun. Ernest's stories, whether set against a sun-drenched Spanish bullring or the bleak trenches of the Italian front, were imbued with the authenticity of his experiences and the passions that defined his existence.

Each of his loves created experiences and feelings that became his novels. The women of his life became fictional characters that we, as regular laymen, will never forget. Lady Duff Twysden became Lady Brett in *The Sun Also Rises*, and Agnes inspired *A Farewell to Arms*. Pauline represents aspects of many of his more well-to-do women in *To Have and Have Not*, *The Short Happy Life of Francis Macomber*, and more. His muse in the young Adrianna became Renata in *Across the River and Into the Trees*.

I am fascinated by the accounts of my grandfather's life, in which he felt the rich were the bane of his (and often his characters') existence. This might be why he continued loving and admiring Hadley throughout his life. They were together before Ernest's success. It was a simple time of hunger, sexual longing, eating or wanting to eat, and a love affair with the city of Paris. Paris in the 1920s was a new world of artists, authors, and intellectuals, and it would not be long before he dominated that world. As highlighted in *A Moveable Feast*, his beginning in Paris was pure and poor, yet his passion for life was at its pinnacle.

Later, my grandfather became a man of means and lived a comfortable lifestyle that allowed him to care for his wives, children, and ex-wives. (The exception was the competitive Martha Gellhorn, who became his nemesis; the two never spoke again after their breakup.) However, the comfortable lifestyle didn't align with him intellectually or emotionally and fueled nothing but frustration—apparent in his later writing.

The Sun Also Rises, *A Farewell to Arms*, *Death in the Afternoon*, *For Whom the Bell Tolls*, and, finally, *The Old Man and the Sea* were all fueled by love, war, grace under pressure, or perhaps all three. Battle inspired most of his work (both the internal battle and the ugly external battle of war). And, of course, he was also deeply inspired by the love he felt for the women he cared about and, from my point of view, by the earth he lived on. In his descriptions of locations, whether Spain, the coast of Cuba, or the French Alps, he depicts light, rivers, trees, and waves in a way that proves nothing short of a love affair with nature. I have always felt that if my grandfather were alive today, he would be a powerful environmentalist in love with nature and, given *his* nature, most likely still in love with some glorious and fabulous woman by his side. If passion was his theme, I see his appreciation of nature as one of his greatest infatuations.

I hope that in these pages, you will find insight into Ernest Hemingway's extraordinary life and a reflection on the enduring power of passion in all its forms.

With profound gratitude, I offer this foreword, a bridge between my understanding of Ernest Hemingway and the man you will come to know in the following chapters. May you discover, as I have, more about this remarkable figure, my family's legacy, and, perhaps, the greatest writer the world has ever known.

Mariel Hemingway
Granddaughter of Ernest Hemingway

Prologue

Figure 1.1. Ernest Hemingway, passport photo 1923.
Ernest Hemingway Collection, John F. Kennedy Presidential Library and Museum, Boston, Massachusetts.

JOURNALIST, ADVENTURER, SPORTSMAN, LOVER—ERNEST HEMINGWAY, the Nobel Prize–winning author, embodied many talents and pursued numerous interests during his legendary lifetime. Every chapter of Hemingway's exceptional life was a fresh adventure, usually with a different romantic partner and in a new location that energized his creativity with new experiences, acquaintances, connections, and perspectives. His life formed a series of concentric circles, always moving to interesting places to provide content, settings, and inspiration for new novels, short stories, and non-fiction articles.

Ernest's personal experiences became the content of his writing. He developed plots from his adventures, used details from places he lived or visited to create settings, and formed characters based on friends and acquaintances he met along the way. It was dangerous to be Ernest's friend because he frequently transformed "friends" into controversial characters in one of his novels or short stories.

Ernest's first passion was writing, but he also was an adventurer, an outdoorsman, and a keen observer of people. He purposely sought dangerous situations to test his own levels of courage and to discover models for literary heroes that displayed grace under pressure. He tested his physical endurance and courage by skiing through trees, hunting big game in Africa, and even facing bulls in the ring.

"Grace under pressure" was a behavior he studied throughout his life and was demonstrated by his literary heroes, regardless of whether they were facing a wartime enemy, a charging bull, or a great marlin. Ernest defined grace under pressure while skiing in Schruns, Austria, with Gerald Murphy and John Dos Passos. Skiing through trees toward the base of the mountain required the men to not only negotiate the snow and the pitch of the terrain, but also navigate through the trees. Even though Ernest stopped often to check on their well-being, Gerald Murphy and John Dos Passos were terrified by the experience. Ernest, however, found the adventure exhilarating and told his friends, "He knew what courage was. It was grace under pressure." He felt "absolutely elated."[1]

As time passed, Ernest not only sought adventures that challenged his physical safety, but also his emotional safety. His risk-taking behavior impacted his personal relationships, but his masculine adventurous spirit appealed to women of all ages, including four wives and a long list of legendary actresses.

He was born in 1899, raised in Victorian-era Oak Park, Illinois, but hungered to understand the challenges and actions needed to live in an ever-changing world. He didn't let social conventions stand in his way and fought for his beliefs and wrote about his values. His heroism in the trenches during World War I earned him the Italian medaglia d'argento a valore. His willingness to enter combat areas under fire during World War II earned him a Bronze Star. His courage to write about the good, the bad, and the ugly brought him a Nobel Prize and the Pulitzer Prize for Literature.

Ernest's tenacity and spirit of adventure were cultivated by his parents and grandfathers as well as the spouses and companions he chose to befriend throughout his life. As a toddler, Ernest told his mother that he was "friad of nothing" and that "When I get to be a big boy . . . I want to go with Dad and shoot lions and wolves."[2] He was born and spent the first eighteen years of his life in suburban Oak Park, Illinois, but spent each of those summers at the family cottage in northern Michigan. There he developed a need for adventure and learned the skills necessary to meet and enjoy the challenges of hunting and fishing.

Ernest's father nurtured his son's love of the outdoors, his skills as a marksman, and his love of water. Dr. Hemingway longed to be a medical missionary but settled for a medical practice in Oak Park and summers spent hunting and fishing in Michigan. He was medical examiner for three insurance companies and the Borden Milk Company as well as head of obstetrics at Oak Park Hospital, and during his career he delivered more than three thousand babies.[3]

As a youth, Clarence Hemingway spent three influential months with the Sioux Indians of South Dakota and developed great admiration for American Indian traditions and culture. As an adult, he won the respect of local Chippewa (Ojibwe) tribes that worked in the Michigan logging industry. American Indians were housed in camps that surrounded the Hemingway cottage, and Dr. Hemingway provided pro bono medical services to the injured and the sick. He also earned the name Ne-teck-ta-la or Eagle Eye because of his excellent marksmanship.

3

Figure 1.2. Ernest Hemingway at eighteen months, January 1901.
"friad of nothing."
Marcelline Hemingway Sanford photographs. Ernest Hemingway Foundation
of Oak Park Archives, Oak Park Public Library Special Collections, Oak Park,
Illinois.

Dr. Hemingway's knowledge of the natural world influenced Ernest's lifelong love of hunting and fishing, but it also permeated his writing. The memories of times Ernest spent with his father appear in the Nick Adams stories. In "Indian Camp," Nick Adams and his doctor father row across a lake to a nearby Indian camp. Nick's father has been called to deliver a woman who has been in labor for two days. At the camp, they find the woman screaming in pain, lying on a bottom bunkbed; her husband lies above her with a foot injured in a logging accident. To Nick's amazement and shock, his father performs a Caesarian with a jack-knife and sews the woman up with fishing line. After the baby is delivered, Nick's father turns to help the woman's husband on the top bunk and finds that he fatally slit his own throat with a razor. The story ends with Nick and his father on the lake, rowing away from the camp.

Nick, like Ernest, takes comfort in the companionship of his father. "They were seated in the boat, Nick in the stern, his father rowing. The sun was coming up over the hills. A bass jumped, making a circle in the water. Nick trailed his hand in the water. It felt warm in the sharp chill of the morning."[4] As they are rowing across the lake, Nick asks his father if dying is hard. His father says, "No, I think it's pretty easy," and Nick concludes that "In the early morning on the lake sitting is the stern of the boat with his father rowing . . . he would never die."[5]

Ernest also remembered his father and life at Walloon Lake in his short story "Fathers and Sons." He used his own experiences and feelings about hunting and fishing with his father to develop the main character, Nick Adams, saying,

> someone has to give you your first gun or the opportunity to get it and use it, and you have to live where there is game or fish if you are to learn about them, and now, at thirty-eight, he loved to fish and to shoot exactly as much as when he first had gone with his father. It was a passion that had never slackened and he was very grateful to his father for bringing him to know it.[6]

He would go on to say that, "His father came back to him in the fall of the year, or in the early spring when there had been jacksnipe on the prairie, or when he saw shocks of corn, or when the saw a lake or . . . heard wild geese, or in a duck blind."[7]

Dr. Hemingway taught Ernest to hunt, fish, and love the outdoors, but also to understand and respect the dangers inherent in the natural world. The Hemingway children were allowed to have guns at an early age, but Clarence Hemingway understood their potential danger and advised that, "Accidents don't happen to people who know how to handle guns. . . . Treat a gun like a friend. Keep it clean. Oil it, clean it after every use, but always remember, it's an enemy if it's carelessly used."[8]

Dr. Hemingway's lessons in "safety" also cultivated Ernest's need for excitement and adventure. During the summers in Michigan, Dr. Hemingway held lifesaving drills during which he took his children into deep water, deliberately rocked the boat until it capsized, and forced his children to "Swim for Shore!"[9] Ernest and his siblings found their father's lifesaving drills exciting, were keen about the competitive swimming races to shore, and, at a young age, learned to exercise "grace under pressure."

Usually, the family prepared for the summer in Michigan by leaving the Oak Park home, boarding the SS *Manitou*, and traveling three hundred miles north on Lake Michigan to Harbor Springs, Michigan. From there, they traveled by train to Petoskey and then to Walloon Village and again by boat to the house on Walloon Lake. However, an exception was made to this travel plan in the summer of 1917 when only the Hemingway girls traveled to Walloon Lake by steamer. Though there were no gas stations, few hotels, and mostly unpaved roads, Ernest, his father, his mother, and his younger brother, Leicester, made the summer journey in the new family car, a Ford Model T touring car. The 487-mile journey took five days. The family camped in tents at night and brought along a saw so that Ernest could cut branches to provide traction for the car on the sandy roads of northern Michigan.

Ernest's mother, Grace Hall Hemingway, made the trip in the Model T and embraced life in Michigan, but she also liked to think of herself as an English gentlewoman. Her parents emigrated from England and eventually built the Queen Anne house with a turret and six bedrooms in Oak Park. Grace grew up in that house, then raised the first four of her six children there. In Oak Park she followed the English tradition of

Figure 1.3. Hemingway family at Walloon Lake, July 1915.
Back row standing: Marcelline and Ernest. Middle row standing: Madelaine and Ursula. Front row standing: Clarence holding Carol and Grace holding Leicester.

Marcelline Hemingway Sanford photographs. Ernest Hemingway Foundation of Oak Park Archives, Oak Park Public Library Special Collections, Oak Park, Illinois.

Figure 1.4. Hemingway's birthplace home: 439 N. Oak Park Avenue, Oak Park, Illinois. *Marcelline Hemingway Sanford photographs. Ernest Hemingway Foundation of Oak Park Archives, Oak Park Public Library Special Collections, Oak Park, Illinois.*

Figure 1.5. The Hemingways arrive in Michigan by car, 1917. *Marcelline Hemingway Sanford photographs. Ernest Hemingway Foundation of Oak Park Archives, Oak Park Public Library Special Collections, Oak Park, Illinois.*

Figure 1.6. Grace Hall Hemingway showing Ernest and his sisters, Marcelline and Ursula, the seven-pound pike she caught.
Ernest Hemingway Foundation of Oak Park Archives, Oak Park Public Library Special Collections, Oak Park, Illinois.

celebrating Boxing Day and was a member of the Nineteenth Century Woman's Club and the Oak Park Art League, but she also embraced life at the isolated Michigan cottage she called Windermere, which was lit only by oil lamps and heated with a fireplace. While she loved music and organized a family orchestra in the parlor of her Oak Park home, she also had her own .22 rifle, fished for pike and lake trout in Michigan, and nurtured her son's love of the outdoors. A few weeks before his third birthday, she wrote, "Ernest shoots well with his gun and loads it and cocks it himself . . . and 'has wonderful courage and endurance' while fishing at Windermere."[10]

Grace loved music and had a beautiful voice. After high school, she trained for opera with Madame Louisa Cappianni in New York and gave

Figure 1.7. Ernest, age four, with his gun near Windemere Cottage at Walloon Lake, Michigan.
Ernest Hemingway Collection. John F. Kennedy Presidential Library and Museum, Boston, Massachusetts.

Figure 1.8. Ernest, age four, fishing near Windemere Cottage at Walloon Lake. *Ernest Hemingway Collection. John F. Kennedy Presidential Library and Museum, Boston, Massachusetts.*

a recital at Madison Square Garden but was bothered by the glaring footlights and decided to return to Oak Park and marry Clarence Hemingway, who then moved to Grace's family's home. Grace continued to pursue her interest in music by giving voice lessons and organizing the church choirs. However, when her father died, she used her inheritance to build her forty-five-hundred-square-foot dream home.

Ernest's 1906 "boyhood home" reflects the prairie-style influence of neighbor and architect Frank Lloyd Wright, who lived in Oak Park from 1889 to 1909, and exhibits the typical Prairie-style features of overhanging eaves and stucco façades with horizonal wood trim. The fifteen-room house included a thirty-by-thirty-foot music room with a two-story high balcony for recitals and concerts. When the new house was finished, the family held a small ceremony to light the fire on the hearthstone.

Marcelline and Ernest sang two songs, and then the house was blessed and dedicated to a happy family life.

The music room was Grace's joy, and the tradition of family concerts continued. When Grace decided a cello was needed to provide depth for performances, Ernest was given a cello and required to practice a half hour a day, eventually graduating to a full hour of daily practice. According to his brother, Leicester, Ernest later attributed the tedious practice sessions to the initiation of his writing career. When people would ask him how he got started writing, his stock answer was: "Part of my success, I owe to the hours when I was alone in the music room and was supposed to be practicing. I'd be doing my thinking while playing 'Pop Goes the Weasel' over and over again."[11]

Grace was excited to build her dream home and leave the house she had been living in since the age of fifteen, but Ernest later reflected on the move to the new house with some bitterness. In preparation for the move to the new house, Grace got rid of her parents' old Victorian furniture and moved only her mother's oil paintings, her father's books, and her piano. She burned what she considered clutter, including the medical specimens that her husband kept in jars in the circular attic room of the turret. Ernest thought the purge of his father's specimens was insensitive and later recalled in "Now I Lay Me,"

> I remembered, after my grandfather died we moved away from that house to a new house designed and built by my mother. Many things that were not to be moved were burned in the backyard. And I remember those jars from the attic being thrown into the fire, and how they popped in the heat and the fire flamed up from the alcohol.[12]

Though Ernest's maternal grandfather died when he was six, both grandfathers were veterans of the Civil War, and his paternal grandfather, Anson Hemingway, continued to inspire Ernest's belief that war was the venue for men to display courage and honor. Anson served in the Civil War in the 72nd Illinois Infantry Division. He enlisted in 1862 when he was only seventeen, was commissioned as a first lieutenant in 1864, and was honorably discharged in 1866. He fought in the battle at Vicksburg and wrote in his war journal that "This place is very strongly fortified and it will cost a man a life to take it—but it must fall. We must take it."[13] Anson's half-brothers also fought in the Civil War. Only Anson returned alive.

As Ernest grew up, he observed Grandfather Anson proudly wearing his Civil War uniform, displaying his medals, and marching with his comrades in the yearly Oak Park Memorial Day parades. From him, Ernest inherited an extraordinary sense of pride from wearing a uniform, a great sense of honor from receiving medals, and a lifelong interest in military action. When the United States entered World War I in April 1917, Ernest couldn't wait to get involved. Though he couldn't enlist due to poor eyesight, he eventually went to Italy as a Red Cross ambulance driver, fully embracing the teachings of his grandfathers.

Given the early influences of his grandfathers, Ernest had a lifelong compulsion to take part, observe, and write about the strategies, actions, and consequences of war. He left home and forsook a college education to become a Red Cross volunteer in Italy during World War I and later left Paris, spending four days and three nights on the Orient Express to Constantinople, to cover the Greco-Turkish War for the *Toronto Star*. His fascination with war and his firsthand experiences inspired vivid reports for the paper. As the Greek peasants exited Thrace, he described the "silent, ghastly procession" of displaced humanity, observing the "exhausted, staggering men, women and children, blankets over their heads, walking blindly along in the rain beside their worldly goods."[14] When he returned to Paris in the fall of 1922, he was taking quinine to reduce his fever and his head was shaved because of sleeping in lice-infested beds.

Throughout his life, Ernest studied the tactical aspects of battles and observed and recorded how men faced difficult situations and death. His desire to test his own courage and observe others in life-threatening situations forced him to seek assignments as a war correspondent during the Spanish Civil War and World War II. Though the experiences of modern warfare caused him to reevaluate the teachings of his grandfathers, his interest in warfare inspired two of his bestselling war novels, *A Farewell to Arms* and *For Whom the Bell Tolls*.

The values of Ernest's grandparents and parents were consistent and clear. The grandparents focused service to God and to their country; the parents prided themselves on their interest in church missionary work and the fine arts. They supported movements, ranging from the establishment of nature study groups, including the establishment of the local branch of the Agassiz Society, to Protestant missionary groups dedicated to spreading the Word around the world.

Christian religious principles, a traditional education in public schools, and a strong work ethic were imparted to Ernest as a child and nurtured via frequent letters after he left Oak Park. As a child, Ernest was expected to be doing something useful. Dr. Hemingway had no patience for just sitting around or relaxing in a chair and had little room for compromise between what he considered right and wrong. Dr. Hemingway believed social dancing, card playing, and gambling were wrong, and forbade smoking and drinking alcoholic beverages. If his children did something wrong, they were either sent to their rooms without supper or spanked with a razor strop. After the punishment, they were to kneel and ask God for forgiveness.

Though Ernest was influenced by his parents and grandparents, as time passed, he developed an autonomous morality, in which his personal standards were different from those of his parents. After graduation from high school, Ernest moved to Kansas City and got a job as a cub reporter for the *Kansas City Star*. His parents wanted him to go to college, but his high school experiences convinced him he had the talent to be a writer.

Ernest's publication efforts were encouraged by his high school journalism teacher, Fannie Biggs. Miss Biggs conducted her classroom as though it were a newspaper room, with rotating editors and daily assignments of news stories, sporting events, and advertising. Miss Biggs taught her students there were three criteria for a good article: "Tell your whole story in the first paragraph; develop details in relation to their importance; leave the least important things till the end because the editor may have to cut."[15]

In high school, Ernest learned the importance of observation and the power of writing about personal experiences. His first article, "Concert a Success," appeared in the school newspaper, *Trapeze*, in the January 20,

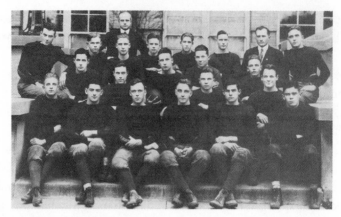

Figure 1.9. Oak Park High School Football Team 1915, Oak Park, Illinois. Ernest—front row, second from right.
Marcelline Hemingway Sanford photographs. Ernest Hemingway Foundation of Oak Park Archives, Oak Park Public Library Special Collections, Oak Park, Illinois.

1916, issue, and reported on a performance that the Chicago Symphony Orchestra had given in Oak Park. By the time Ernest left high school, he had recounted his running for a touchdown on the school's football team in the sports column, had the experience of being editor of the *Trapeze*, and had published three short stories set in Northern Michigan in the school's literary magazine, *Tabula*. As the sportswriter for the paper, he detailed a football game, saying, "Hemingway went over for the first touchdown by way of the Lake Street 'L.'"[16] As the author of the short story, "Judgment of Manitou," he reflected on life in Michigan by developing a conflict between two Canadian trappers, Dick Haywood and his half French and half Cree partner, Pierre. When Pierre suspects that Dick has stolen his wallet, he plots revenge in a murder in which Dick is caught in a bear trap and killed by timber wolves. As the story progresses, Pierre is lying on a cot in their cabin and sees a red squirrel chewing on the wallet. Pierre rushes out of the cabin to save his friend only to find bloody snow and a raven picking at the shapeless something that had once been his partner. Pierre then becomes the victim of his own plot as he steps into the open bear trap that Haywood had come to tend. Realizing it's the judgment of Manitou, Pierre kills himself with his own rifle.

MADELEINE HANCOCK

Glee Club (3) (4); Opera (3); Atalanta (2) (3) (4); French Club (3) (4); Girls' Club (3) (4).

"As smooth as the business side of a banana peel."

WARD BELMONT

WILBUR HAUPT

Glee Club (2) (3); Opera (2); German Play (2); Athletic Association (4); Boys' High school Club (3) (4); Hanna Club (3).

"Cheeks like roses."

ILLINOIS

ERNEST HEMINGWAY

Class Prophet; Orchestra (1) (2) (3); Trapeze Staff (3), Editor (4); Class Play; Burke Club (3) (4); Athletic Association (1) (2) (4); Boys' High School Club (3) (4); Hanna Club (1) (3) (4); Boys' Rifle Club (1) (2) (3); Major Football (4); Minor Football (2) (3); Track Manager (4); Swimming (4).

"None are to be found more clever than Ernie."

ILLINOIS

MARCELLINE HEMINGWAY

Commencement Speaker; Orchestra (1) (2) (3) (4); Glee Club (3) (4); Tabula Board (4); Trapeze Staff (3), Editor (4); Opera (1) (2) (3); Atalanta (1) (2) (3) (4); Girls' Rifle Club (2) (3) (4); Commercial Club (4); Drama Club (3) (4); Girls' Club (3), Council (4); Story Club (3).

"I'd give a dollar for one of your dimples, Marc."

OBERLIN

Figure 1.10. Ernest's graduation photo and yearbook entry, Oak Park High School, 1917.
Ernest Hemingway Foundation of Oak Park Archives, Oak Park Public Library Special Collections, Oak Park, Illinois.

When Ernest finished high school, he had the confidence and experience to pursue writing as a career. In the summer of 1917, Ernest's Uncle (Alfred) Tyler Hemingway arranged an October interview with Henry Haskell, Uncle Tyler's Oberlin classmate and the chief editorial writer for the *Kansas City Star*. Given a thirty-day trial period at fifteen dollars a week, Ernest moved to Kansas City and initiated a series of adventures that broadened his personal experiences beyond those of Oak Park and Walloon Lake. Ernest's self-confidence, big smile, and boyish good looks enabled him to make friends easily. He was attracted to older writers such as Lionel Moise, who had a reputation as a "lady's man," was a heavy drinker, and was considered a no-nonsense reporter who admired the works of Mark Twain and Joseph Conrad.

Ernest expanded his peer group with older, influential reporters and took opportunities to explore his love of action and adventure at Fifteenth Street, Number 4 Police Station and the General Hospital. His boss, Pete Wellington, has said, "He liked action. . . . He always wanted to be on the scene himself" and recalled that Ernest would take off in hospital ambulances without letting the city desk know where he was going or he'd cover crime at the Fifteenth Street station hoping something larger would hit.[17]

In Kansas City, Ernest began to understand the thrill that came from meeting new people and exploring new places. He expanded his territory and his awareness of the world to Wyoming Street and covered pool halls and dance halls, where prostitutes did business and drug sales were rampant, and to the railroad yards, where he encountered railroad bums living in boxcars. For Ernest, these new experiences fulfilled the old expression that, "Kansas City is a place where boys become men."

Another new friend was Ted Brumback, who had served in France as an ambulance driver before working at the *Star*. Like many young men of their generation, Ernest and Ted were drawn to the action of the war in Europe. Though Ernest eventually credited The *Kansas City Star*'s style manual, which promoted the use of short sentences, short paragraphs, and vigorous English, as "the best rules I ever learned for the business of writing," when Red Cross officials came to Kansas City, Ernest and Brumback quickly signed up to serve as ambulance drivers in

Figure 1.11. The Hemingway family poses for a portrait before Ernest goes to Italy. Oak Park, Illinois, 1918. L–R: Clarence Hemingway, Carol Hemingway, Grace Hall Hemingway, Ernest Hemingway, Leicester Hemingway, Ursula Hemingway, Madelaine "Sunny" Hemingway, and Marcelline Hemingway. *Marcelline Hemingway Sanford photographs. Ernest Hemingway Foundation of Oak Park Archives, Oak Park Public Library Special Collections, Oak Park, Illinois.*

Italy.[18] Earlier, Ernest had written to his sister, Marcelline, "I can't let a show like this go on without getting in on it."[19] Despite his bad left eye, his dream of getting involved with the war was realized.

After picking up his final paycheck, Ernest left Kansas City and went to Oak Park to say goodbye to his family, to Michigan for some fishing, and to his high school to see Miss Biggs. He told her, "If it comes to a death notice for me, I want you to write it, because you'd tell it the way it was, and no gushing."[20]

Mid-May 1918, Ernest boarded the French Line ship *Chicago* in New York for a ten-day passage to Bordeaux and then went on to Paris by train. When Ernest arrived, Paris was being shelled by the Germans, but he didn't let that stop him from continuing to expand his world. He visited Napoleon's tomb, the Hotel des Invalides, the Arc de Triomphe, the Champs-Elysees, the Tuileries, as well as the Follies Bergere. Then on June 6, he boarded a train with other Red Cross volunteers at Gare de Lyon for Milan.

With his arrival in Milan, Ernest was initiated into the disasters of war. An explosion in a munitions factory resulted in Red Cross volunteers being rushed to the scene. According to Milford Baker, another volunteer, "The first thing we saw was the body of a woman, legs gone, head gone, intestines strung out. Hemmie and I nearly passed out cold but gritted our teeth and laid the thing on the stretcher."[21] Later Ernest would use his "search (of) the immediate vicinity and surrounding fields for bodies" in *Death in the Afternoon* in "The Natural History of the Dead."[22]

In Milan, Ernest was assigned to Section Four, the Red Cross ambulance unit in Schio about four miles from the Austrian border. He oversaw a relief station located behind the lines in a battered farmhouse in in the southeast sector at Fossalta di Piave, an area that had seen much damage. At the canteen, soldiers could get hot food and relax, but Ernest also was responsible for bringing chocolate and cigarettes to the Italian soldiers at the front.

It was on a trip to the frontlines on July 8, 1918, that Ernest was injured near Fossalta, Italy, by an exploding Austrian mortar shell while passing out American Red Cross canteen supplies to Italian soldiers. According to his friend Bill Horne,

Ernie grew restless, borrowed a bike and got to the front. He was at an advanced post—a hole in the ground—when the Austrians discovered it and sent over a Minenwerfer. It landed right smack on target. One man was killed, another badly hurt, and Ernie was hit by scaggia (shell fragments). He dragged out his wounded companion, hoisted him on his back and headed for the trenches a hundred yards away. The Austrians turned their machine guns on him and he took a slug under his knee and another in the ankle but he made it. However, he was stiff legged ever after. No one knew who he was as he lay in the surgical post. Then another ambulance driver came along and identified him.[23]

The explosion knocked Ernest unconscious and buried him in dirt. One Italian was instantly killed, another had both his legs blown off, and a third Italian was badly wounded. After Ernest regained consciousness, he put the wounded Italian on his back and carried him to the first aid dugout. Ernest's wounds were dressed in Fornaci. Then he was transported to a field hospital in Treviso and after several days to the American Red Cross Hospital in Milan.

The Italian government awarded Ernest with the medaglia d'argento al valore, citing that he was "Gravely wounded by numerous pieces of shrapnel from an enemy shell, with an admirable spirit of brotherhood, before taking care of himself, he rendered generous assistance to the Italian soldiers more seriously wounded by the same explosion and did not allow himself to be carried elsewhere until after they had been evacuated."[24] When his parents learned of his injury and bravery, Dr. Hemingway wrote, "I do hope and pray you will speedily recover . . . Dear Mother gets more proud of you every day and hour."[25]

Ernest went to Italy looking for adventure and got more than he had bargained for. War revealed itself to the young ambulance driver not only as a venue for heroism for which one gained medals and recognition, but also as a sordid bloodbath where one was required to carry parts of dead bodies and sustain injuries that would last a lifetime. Ernest was hoping to display the honor and courage his grandfathers had talked about but was blown up in a trench. He learned that modern warfare was different from what Grandfather Anson had experienced. After being immersed in a world different from Oak Park and Walloon Lake, he understood new actions and new ways of thinking were required. His experiences in Italy changed Ernest's worldview but also helped to understand and shape it. Surviving in this world required new actions that trumped some of the religious teachings of his parents and some of the manners and morals he learned in Oak Park.

As a result of the horrors of the war, Ernest now encountered a world filled with people who felt betrayed by their leaders, their culture, and their institutions. The experiences in Italy forged a new philosophy of life, one that didn't exist and wasn't needed in Oak Park. Ernest began to develop what eventually would be called the Hemingway Code. Behind the formulation of this concept was the basic disillusionment brought by the war and the realization that the old concepts and values embedded in Christianity and other ethical systems of the Western world had not served to save mankind from the catastrophes inherent in the war. As these actions and rituals evolved, Ernest created a set of rules needed for survival in the post–World War I world and began writing about modern heroes who faced death without the comfort of religion or engaging in self-pity. Through their actions, Ernest's heroes exhibited grace under pressure.

His early short stories, collected in *in our time* and *Men Without Women*, and first novel, *The Sun Also Rises*, were viewed by some as the "sordid little catastrophes in the lives of very vulgar people."[26] However, the criticism of these early works was based on Ernest's honest portrayal of life in the 1920s and the critics' misunderstanding of his old Midwestern values. While he tried to honestly portray the prostitutes, drug fiends, and the rotten crowd of Montparnasse, he had an underlying disdain for the behavior of the rotten crowd, a disdain that was symptomatic of his conservative upbringing.

The 1924 edition of *in our time* consisted of vignettes that centered on World War I news stories, a piece about a robbery and murder in Kansas City that was based on a newspaper story Ernest had covered at the *Kansas City Star*, as well as the story of the public hanging of the Chicago mobster Sam Cardinelli.

Ernest's parents were shocked by the content of his early work. When his father read *in our time*, he was enraged and said he would not tolerate such filth in his house. He told one of his friends that he would rather see Ernest dead than write about such seamy subjects and returned the shipment of books he had ordered to the Paris publisher. When Ernest's first novel, *The Sun Also Rises*, captured the promiscuity and mindless drinking of the Montparnasse crowd Ernest had met in Paris, his mother told him he had produced "one of the filthiest books of the year."[27]

His parents' reaction to his writing was hurtful, and he tried to bridge the gap with an explanatory letter home. Writing to his father from Paris in 1925, he said,

> You see I'm trying in all my stories to get the feeling of actual life—not to just depict life—or criticize it—but to actually make it alive. So that when you have read something by me you actually experience the thing. You can't do this without putting the bad and the ugly as well as what is beautiful. Because if it is all beautiful you can't believe in it. Things aren't that way. It is only by showing both sides—3 dimensions and if possible 4 that you can write the way I want to.[28]

Ernest dared to be different. Compared to Oak Park and Walloon Lake, it was a sordid little world, and the reaction to his "vulgar people" was eventually positive. His critics would write that, "Hemingway's people were immoral, drank too much, had no religion or ideals, [but] have courage and friendship, and mental honestness. And they are alive. Amazingly real and alive."[29] Once he left Oak Park, he discovered a new world that was inhabited by people he never would have met in Oak Park. He seemed to have a need to show his readers what he had told his sister. "There's a whole big world out there full of people who really feel things."[30]

The revolutionary content of *The Sun Also Rises* catapulted Ernest to instant fame at the age of twenty-six. However, he also was praised for the economic style of his writing. Because he knew the old rules, he was able to break them. He understood the boredom that came from endless description, and he didn't tell his readers what to think. He developed a style whereby his code heroes spoke and acted according to a new code of behavior. It was up to the reader to understand them through their actions and dialogue and without endless explanation. Reading the work of Mark Twain, Ernest had discovered the value of dialogue and honest language. He came to believe that all American literature began with *Huckleberry Finn*.

However, breaking the old rules didn't mean one could be careless. His powers of observation were sharpened by his experiences in journalism, and his understanding of grammar and usage honed by Miss Biggs and the standards set by the *Kansas City Star*. Eventually, Ernest settled on what he called "the principle of the iceberg." When talking about the way in which he wrote, he said,

> There is seven eights of it under water for every part that shows. Anything you know you can eliminate, and it only strengthens your iceberg. . . . So I have tried to eliminate everything unnecessary to conveying experience to the reader so that after he or she has read something it will become a part of his or her experience and seem actually to have happened. This is very hard to do and I've worked at it very hard.[31]

Exploring the world beyond Oak Park remained important throughout his life, and Ernest traveled anywhere to create an interesting article, short story, or novel. His life took a miraculous path of discovery. In his twenties, he was exploring new ways of writing with Ezra Pound, Gertrude Stein, and T. S. Eliot in Paris, but he'd also leave France to ski in Switzerland or attend bullfights in Spain. By the time he was thirty, he was savoring the success of his first novels in Key West, Florida, but also fishing for four-hundred-pound marlin in the Gulf Stream or charting a course to Cuba in his new boat. Along the way, he met women who were attracted to his athletic good looks, his storytelling, and his quest for excitement. His life was an adventure, and his writing was revolutionary. He became a legend who shared his discoveries about life as well as his feelings about and experiences with the women he loved with readers around the world, regardless of how shocking his readers or the women he loved might find them.

Agnes

Figure 2.1. Agnes von Kurowsky, Milan, Italy, 1918.
She had gray-blue eyes, long chestnut-colored hair, and a comfortable, if not flirta-tious, manner with men.
Ernest Hemingway Collection. John F. Kennedy Presidential Library and Museum, Boston, Massachusetts.

THE WAR EXPERIENCE IN ITALY WAS AN ADVENTURE THAT CHANGED Ernest's life. In addition to his confrontation with death and his subsequent wound, he had his first experiences with love, infidelity, and heartbreak. While in the American Red Cross hospital in Milan, Ernest met Agnes von Kurowsky, an American who had trained as a nurse in New York and upon graduation applied for overseas duty in Italy. She had gray-blue eyes, long chestnut-colored hair, and a comfortable, if not flirtatious, manner with men.

Agnes von Kurowsky Stanfield was born on January 5, 1892, in Germantown, Philadelphia, Pennsylvania. Her father was a civil service language instructor for the US Army. Her family moved many times, and she cultivated a taste for excitement and adventure at an early age. Living in Alaska, she experienced dog sleds pulled by reindeer and narrowly escaped death from diphtheria. She learned early that life was unpredictable and watched her sister die from complications of scarlet fever and her father succumb to typhoid fever.

After attending the Fairmont Seminary and a training program for the Washington Public Library, she found working in a library "too slow and uneventful" and looked for "something more exciting."[1] She enrolled in the Bellevue Nurses Training Program in New York City, graduated in 1917, and applied for service with the American Red Cross. Her application said she was five feet, eight inches tall, 133 pounds, and fluent in French and German. On June 15, 1918, at the age of twenty-six, she sailed for Le Harve aboard *La Lorraine*. She visited Paris and arrived in Milan on July 11, 1918. There, she took her baggy, ill-fitting Red Cross nurse uniforms to a local tailor to be tightened and shortened, enrolled in Italian lessons, and began her nursing duties.

The American Red Cross Hospital was housed in an elegant stone mansion and filled with classic furniture polished to a soft luster. It was located at 10 Via Mazzoni in the La Scala district, near the Duomo and the Galleria. The fourth floor contained fifteen private rooms for patients. Some of the rooms had balconies, others had wide terraces, and all had views of the summer greenery that surrounded the hospital. The terraces were protected by striped awnings, which were rolled up and down to protect patients from the summer sun. The balconies and balustrades

Figure 2.2. Ernest Hemingway, American Red Cross ambulance driver and recipient of the medaglia d'argento al valore.
Ernest Hemingway Collection. John F. Kennedy Presidential Library and Museum, Boston, Massachusetts.

Figure 2.3. Ernest Hemingway, American Red Cross ambulance driver, Fossalta di Piave, Italy, 1918.

"I can't let a show like this go on without getting in on it."

Ernest Hemingway Collection. John F. Kennedy Presidential Library and Museum, Boston, Massachusetts.

were decorated with flower boxes and potted palms. Patients convalesced in large wicker chairs or chaise lounges and had their meals brought to them.

The nurses' quarters were one floor below. Nurses had their own dining room and kitchen and were required to follow strict rules: Dates were to be chaperoned and even simple errands were to be done in pairs. Agnes followed the rules.

When Ernest arrived on July 17, he had a machine gun slug in his right foot, another behind his right kneecap, and hundreds of steel fragments lodged in his legs. He was swathed in bandages, but despite his injuries, Ernest was in good spirits. He told his parents:

> This is a peach of a hospital here and there are about 18 nurses to take care of 4 patients. Everything is fine and I am very comfortable and one of the best surgeons in Milan is looking after my wounds. There are a couple of pieces still in. One bullet in my knee that the Xray showed. The surgeon, very wisely after consultation, is going to wait for the wound in my right knee to become healed cleanly before operating. The bullet will then be rather encysted, and he will make a clean cut and go in under the side of the knee cap. By allowing it to be completely healed first he thus avoids any danger of infection and stiff knee. This is wise don't you think, Dad?[2]

Amused by his injuries, Ernest entertained his friends from Section Four by prying out the imbedded steel fragments from his legs with a pen knife and joked with his family that he would "never look well in kilts," but his brush with death had an impact on his outlook on life and the content of his writing.[3] He had encountered death, faced danger, endured pain, and behaved with courage. By saving the life of an unknown Italian soldier, he became a hero; the attention he received only increased his self-confidence. Now he was not only attractive to women and respected by men but also formally decorated as a hero by the Italian government. When he was taken outside the hospital to review a parade, he was treated as the American hero of the Piave by the local Italians. He told his family:

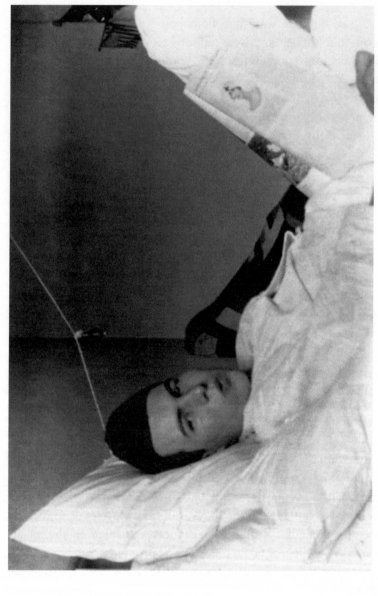

Figure 2.4. Ernest Hemingway, American Red Cross Hospital, Milan, Italy, 1918. "Wounded 227 times."

Ernest Hemingway Foundation of Oak Park Archives Oak Park Public Library Special Collections, Oak Park, Illinois.

Figure 2.5. Ernest Hemingway recovering at the American Red Cross Hospital, Milan, Italy, 1918.
"Dear Mother gets more proud of you every day and hour."
Ernest Hemingway Collection. John F. Kennedy Presidential Library and Museum, Boston, Massachusetts.

Figure 2.6. Ernest and Agnes on the terrace of the American Red Cross Hospital, Milan, Italy, 1918.
"He is adorable, and we are congenial in every way."
Ernest Hemingway Collection. John F. Kennedy Presidential Library and Museum, Boston, Massachusetts.

With a bodyguard of about six Italian officers I sat on the plaza and reviewed the troops. The crowds cheered me for about ten solid minutes, and I had to take off my cap and bow about 50 times. They threw flowers all over me and every body wanted to shake my hand and the girls all wanted my name so they could write to me. The master journalist was known to the crowd as the American Hero of the Piave. I'm nothing but a second Lieut. or Soto tenente but all the Captains saluted me first. Oh it was very thrilling. I tried to act very dignified but felt very embarrassed.[4]

Figure 2.7. Ernest and Agnes at the San Siro Racetrack, Milan, 1918.
"I didn't win a cent and lost 30 lire but enjoyed it nevertheless."
Ernest Hemingway Collection. John F. Kennedy Presidential Library and Museum, Boston, Massachusetts.

Though he was embarrassed by the attention, he relished receiving medals from the Italian government. He told his family that he had been recommended for the valor medal of the Duke of Aosta, who was the brother of the king, in addition to another recommendation for the silver medal. Then he added that the silver medal is next the highest decoration that any man can receive and that it carried a pension.[5]

Ernest was a handsome hero, a good-natured nineteen-year-old, and the nurses spoiled him. He joked with all of them but quickly became attracted to Agnes. From his hospital bed, he wrote letters to her that she read in the nurses' quarters one floor below. She liked his vitality and spirit of adventure and began to sit with him in his room when she had night duty. She wrote in her diary, "He is adorable, and we are congenial in every way."[6]

The other male patients were attracted to Agnes too, but another patient, Henry Villard noted:

> I knew he had the inside track when I saw him holding her hand one day in a manner that did not suggest she was taking his pulse. I couldn't help noticing that he received an extra share of her attention due partly in the special fondness that seemed to be developing between them.[7]

By September, Ernest had the bullets removed from his leg and his nagging fear of amputation was gone. As he convalesced, Agnes joined him on the balcony outside his room when she finished her duties. After Ernest was fitted with crutches, they went to the horse races and enjoyed candlelight dinners at Gran Italia, but as their relationship grew, Agnes never mentioned she had a doctor-fiancé in New York.

Ernest's family sensed he had a girlfriend. On October 2, 1918, his sister Marcelline sent her "devotion" to his "newest love" and told him he had a talent for "picking winners."[8] Then she questioned in a postscript, "Is it a Red Cross nurse? I won't tell."[9] Ernest responded to his sister's curiosity, saying, "In regard to the question you asked, Yes, she is a Cross Red Nurse" and adds that "Frances Coates and all the others can take a back seat."[10] He tells Marcelline that he doesn't want to "talk about things anymore" and "so guess anything you want to. But I don't wear my heart on my sleeve anymore. But all Oak Park damsels are going to have to show something. I'm off of them the whole bunch. . . . Child, I'm going to stay over here until my girl goes home and then I'll go up north and get rested before I have to go to work in the fall."[11]

Separation came when Ernest was sent to Lake Maggiore for convalescent leave and Agnes was transferred to Florence to nurse an officer with typhoid fever. On October 15, Ernest took Agnes to the train station in a carriage, and they vowed to write frequently. While they were apart, Ernest's feelings for Agnes continued to grow. He wrote to his mother that he was in love, but his real confidant remained Marcelline.

Though Marcelline was nineteen months older than Ernest, Grace had raised Ernest and Marcelline as twins. She held Marcelline back so the siblings went through school together, had common friends, and a close, gossipy friendship. By November 23, Ernest revealed his growing love and secret feelings about Agnes to his sister:

> I don't know what I've written you about my girl but really, Kid Ivory I love her very much. Also she loves me. In fact I love her more than anything or anybody in the world or the world its-self. And Kid I've got a lot clearer look at the world and things than when I was at home. Really Ivory you wouldn't know me I mean to look at or to talk to . . . really Kid I'm immensely older. So when I say that I'm in love with Ag it doesn't mean that I have a case on her. It means that I love her. So believe me or not as you wish. Always I've wondered what it would be like to really meet the girl you will really love always and now I know. Furthermore she loves me—which is quite a miracle in it's self. So don't say anything to the folks because I'm confiding in you. But I'm not foolish and think I can get married now but when I do marry I know who I'm going to marry and if the family don't like it they can lump it and I never will come home. But don't say anything for I'm not going to get married for two years.
>
> Oh Ivory but I love that girl. Now don't ever say I'm not confidential—I've written you what I wouldn't write anybody.[12]

Agnes encouraged Ernest with romantic correspondence. She wrote daily during her three weeks stay in Florence, saying,

> I think everyday how nice it would be to feel your arms around me again. . . . I am so proud of you and the fact that you love me, that I want to blurt it all out. . . . That is our sacrifice, bambino mio, to keep our secrets to ourselves, but so long as you have no secrets from me and I have none from you . . . why should we worry about whether the old world knows.[13]

Her letters were loving but filled with phrases showing her awareness of their seven-year age difference. She called him "kid," "mon enfant," and "dear boy," and she characterized their relationship as a "secret." Did their relationship need to be a secret because she had been his nurse or because she wanted to be available to other men? Maybe she wanted to be independent but liked having a boyfriend too.

When her friend's fiancé was missing in action, she wrote, "Don't let me gain you only to lose you . . . I love you Ernie. . . . In spite of the sunshine I am lost without you. I thought it was the dismal rain that made me miss you so."[14]

When Ernest's knee healed, he was shipped back to the front. He was excited to be back in the action but came down with a severe case of jaundice that forced his return to the hospital. Ernest was hopeful but didn't feel well. Writing to his family, he said:

> Well I might as well tell you why I'm in bed again. Nothing bad. You see I got a leave of absence from the Hospital the day the offensive started and blew for the front. Worked hard day and night where the worst mountain fighting was and then came down with jaundice. It makes you feel rotten and look like an inhabitant of the flowery king-dom but is nothing to worry about. I had the satisfaction of being in the offensive any way and now I can rest up in the hospital and get cured and finish the treatments on my leg.[15]

Agnes reacted to his illness differently. She was excited to learn he had jaundice because she thought they would be reunited in Milan. On the same day as Ernest wrote to his family about feeling rotten, she wrote "I just buried my head in my pillow and laughed for joy to think I am going to see you in Milan when I get back. . . . Dear Kid, hurry up and get well so I shant worry about you. Just imagine yourself kissed goodbye by your own Mrs. Kid, Aggie."[16]

Now that Agnes was signing her letters Mrs. Kid, she finally told Ernest about her doctor fiancé in New York. She admitted that she felt bad about being unfaithful to the doctor and feared that Ernest might think she was fickle and untrustworthy. She told Ernest, "the dreadful thought came to me today that maybe my punishment for this treat-ment of him would be to have you treat me in a like manner someday. I certainly need a dose of your presence, dear, to reassure and comfort me."[17] Then when Ernest mentioned a possible job in Rome, she again voiced concern about trust and questioned, "Will you be in Rome all the time or travelling around Italy? I guess you don't trust me much as you are unwilling to place the old Atlantic between us. I can't very well blame you, seeing what I did to the doctor—Well Ernie my darlin', some day you'll believe in me just as firmly as I now hold my faith in you."[18]

Though they were never reunited in Milan, Agnes continued to give Ernest the impression that someday they would marry. On December 1, she wrote, "I sometimes wish we could marry over here, but since that is so foolish I must try not to think of it."[19] Twelve days later she told him, "I wrote to my mother that I was planning to marry a man younger than I—and it wasn't the doctor so I expect she'll give me up as a hopeless flirt."[20]

When the war ended and Ernest learned he would go home on January 1, aboard the *Giuseppe Verdi* out of Genoa, Agnes was forced to evaluate her true feelings about Ernest. Realistically, she was ambivalent about returning to the United States to marry Ernest. She had not told him she had not officially broken off with the doctor, that she was concerned about their age difference, nor that she loved nursing and being in Europe. She responded, "it makes me shiver to think of your going home without me. What if our hearts should change? and we should lose this beautiful world of us?"[21] Then the next day she wrote "So you are really going . . . can't hardly realize it, but I think you are doing right."[22] She also added that in a few weeks she would be leaving for a ruined section of the Veneto to supervise a small hospital and dispensary, rationalizing "so long as you are not in Italy what diff does it make where I go."[23]

After the Armistice, Ernest returned to New York and then to Oak Park. Bill Horne met Ernest when he disembarked from the *Guiseppe Verde* on New Year's 1919. Now Ernest was a hero, and Horne recalled:

> He was a darn dramatic sight. Over six feet tall, wearing a Bersagllere hat with great cock feathers, an enormous officer's cape lined with red satin, a British-style tunic with ribbons of the Valor Medal and Italian War Cross, and a limp!" The New York Times carried a front-page story and picture, "Most Wounded Hero Returns Home Today," while

the Chicago American noted his return with a headline on page three, "Worst Shot-up Man In US. Is On Way Home."[24]

From New York, Ernest took the train to Chicago. Dr. Hemingway and Marcelline met Ernest at the LaSalle Street Station. When they returned to the Kenilworth Avenue house, a collection of neighbors and friends gave Ernest a hero's welcome. Later, Frank Platt, one of his high school teachers, asked him to speak to the Debate Club, and at a high school assembly, students memorized a welcoming song, singing, "Hemingway, we hail you the victor/Hemingway, ever winning the game." For months, he was in much demand for speaking at local clubs and church groups and was the focus of parties hosted by Italian American organizations.

While in Florence, the frequency of Agnes's letters began to dwindle, perhaps because she had met a handsome Neapolitan who was heir to a dukedom. Though she said nothing about her new suitor, there were hints in her letters. "Cavie has been very cruel to me lately, accusing me of being a flirt."[25] She told Ernest, "You know I don't do anything like that, don't you?" but signed her letter "Affectionately Aggie." Later she wrote, "I'm having the time of my young life," confessed that she was "not the perfect being you think I am," and said that she was "feeling very cattiva [mischievous] tonight."[26] She ended her letter by saying "So good night, kid, and don't do anything rash, but have a good time."[27]

Despite the change in tone and the decreased frequency of letters, when Ernest returned to Oak Park, he still believed he and Agnes would someday marry. But with Ernest gone, Agnes was attracted to others. Eventually, she wrote to her "boy" that she planned to marry another:

Ernie, Dear Boy,

I am writing this late at night after a long think by myself, & I am afraid it is going to hurt you, but, I'm sure it won't harm you permanently.

For quite a while before you left, I was trying to convince myself it was a real love-affair, because, we always seemed to disagree, & then arguments always wore me out so that I finally gave in to keep you from doing something desperate. Now, after a couple of months away from you, I know that I am still very fond of you, but, it is more as a mother than as a sweetheart. It's alright to say I'm a Kid, but, I'm not, & I'm getting less & less so every day.

So, Kid (still Kid to me, & always will be) can you forgive me some day for unwittingly deceiving you? You know I'm not really bad, & don't mean to do wrong, & now I realise it was my fault in the beginning that you cared for me, & regret it from the bottom of my heart. But, I am now & always will be too old, & that's the truth, & I can't get away from the fact that you're just a boy—a kid.

I tried hard to make you understand a bit of what I was thinking on that trip from Padua to Milan, but, you acted like a spoiled child, & I couldn't keep on hurting you. Now, I only have the courage because I'm far away.

Then—& believe me when I say this is sudden for me, too—I expect to be married soon. And I hope & pray that after you thought things out, you'll be able to forgive me & start a wonderful career & show what a man you really are.

Ever admiringly & fondly,
Your friend,
Aggie[28]

Ernest was heart-broken, or to use his word, "smashed." From Oak Park, he wrote to Bill Horne, saying:

I'll tell you the sad truth which I have been suspecting for some time since I've been back and culminated with a letter from Ag this morning.

She doesn't love me Bill. She takes it all back. A "mistake" one of those little mistakes you know. Oh Bill I can't kid about it and I can't be bitter because I'm just smashed by it. And the devil of it is that it wouldn't have happened if I hadn't left Italy. For Christ's sake never leave your girl until you marry her. I know you can't "Learn about wim-men from me" just as I cant learn from any one else. But you, meaning the world in general, . . . you make love to a girl and then you go away. She needs somebody to make love to her. If the right person turns up you're out of luck. That's the way it goes. You won't believe me just as I wouldn't.

Figure 2.8. Ernest Hemingway, recovering from a broken heart outside the
600 N. Kenilworth house, Oak Park, Illinois, 1919.
"All I wanted was Ag and happiness."
*Ernest Hemingway Foundation of Oak Park Archives, Oak Park Public Library
Special Collections, Oak Park, Illinois.*

But Bill I've loved Ag. She's been my ideal and Bill I forgot all about religion and everything else—because I had Ag to worship. Well the crash of smashing ideals was never pretty music to any ones ears. But she doesn't love me now Bill and she is going to marry some one, name not given, whom she has met since. Marry him very soon and she hopes that after I have forgiven her I will start and have a wonderful career and everything.

But Bill I don't want a wonderful career and everything. That isn't really fair she didn't say "and everything." All I wanted was Ag and happiness. And now the bottom has dropped out of the whole world and I'm writing to you with a dry mouth and a lump in the old throat and Bill I wish you were here to talk to. The Dear Kid! I hope he's best man in the world. Aw Bill I can't write about it. Cause I do love her so damned much. . . . I've got to stop before I begin feeling bitter because Im not going to do that I love Ag to much

Write me Kid
Ernie[29]

Though Hemingway, the hero and legend, had been born, the Italian experience not only changed Ernest physically, but also emotionally. Ernest's relationship with Agnes was adventurous, exciting, and painful. Agnes was his first love, and the fact that she was pretty and admired by the other patients but drawn to him was a boost to his already healthy ego and self-confidence. Agnes, too, was adventurous but also mindful of their age difference, and aware of the destruction and uncertainty of war. She was looking for adventure and a flirt, but there is no evidence that her attraction to Ernest was ever sexually consummated.

When Ernest returned to Oak Park, he experienced notoriety but also tremendous sadness. Most of his high school friends were away at college, and he couldn't get a job because the pain in his leg kept him from standing more than a few hours at a time. He confronted a family life that he no longer felt a part of and a set of goals and values he could only partially embrace. Most of his spare time was filled with reading.

The 1925 short story, "A Soldier's Home," delineates Ernest's sense of loss and alienation upon returning to Oak Park after the war. The main character, Krebs, spends his days sleeping in late, walking to the library to get books about the recent war, and practicing his clarinet. He doesn't have a job and tends to watch other people going about their lives. Like Ernest, Krebs feels alienated from everyone in his hometown, including his own parents and the local girls. The initial enthusiasm with which the townspeople greeted him has passed, and like Ernest, Krebs talks about the war, but realizes no one really listens.

Krebs also mirrors the aftermath of Ernest's disastrous relationship with Agnes. Krebs wants a girl but only if he doesn't have to talk to her and form a romantic bond. His strongest relationship is with his sister. Helen is described as his "best sister" and the only girl he has any time for. Like Ernest's parents, Krebs's parents do not tolerate just sitting around. They encouraged him to get back out into the world, start courting, find a job, and make a success of his life.

Agnes was Ernest's first love but not his last love. In time, Ernest moved on to new places and new people. He got back out into the world, started courting, found a job, and made a success of his life. Ten years and two marriages after receiving the devasting letter from Agnes, Ernest immortalized her as Catherine Barkley in *A Farewell to Arms* and shared his unfulfilled personal desires and secrets with his readers.

Few authors have left their desires and fantasies so exposed to posterity. As Catherine, Agnes becomes submissive, lovely, and a compelling vehicle for advancing Ernest's ideas about life, love, and war. Unlike Agnes, Catherine loves only one man. Her fiancé is dead. She also fulfills Ernest's sexual fantasies about Agnes by sleeping with him in the hospital, becoming pregnant by him, and then running off to Switzerland with him.

In writing *A Farewell to Arms*, Ernest followed the advice he eventually gave F. Scott Fitzgerald: "Forget your personal tragedy. We are all bitched from the start and you especially have to hurt like hell before you can write seriously. But when you get the damned hurt use it."[30]

Ernest used his damned hurt to develop a realistic and highly autobiographical account of the war but mixed his personal experiences with his growing disillusionment with war and his romantic fantasies about Agnes. While working with the Italian ambulance service during

World War I, the American lieutenant Frederic Henry meets the English nurse, Catherine Barkley. After Frederic is badly wounded by a trench mortar shell, he is brought to a hospital in Milan, where Catherine eventually joins him and tends to him as he recovers. As their relationship deepens, Frederic falls in love with her, and Catherine becomes pregnant. The novel is divided into five sections, or "books." Frederic Henry narrates the story in the first person.

BOOK ONE

Like Ernest, Lieutenant Frederic Henry is serving as an ambulance driver in the Italian Army during the First World War and is quickly introduced to the realities of war. It is the start of winter when a cholera epidemic kills thousands of soldiers. Initially, Frederic reflects the idealism Ernest learned from his grandfathers. He enters the war with a sense of responsibility and purpose. He believes that the condition of the ambulances depends on him, but realizes after his leave that, "It did not matter whether I was there or not."[31] He tries to do his job properly, but the system works against him. He quickly learns the only way to help the Italian soldier with a rupture is for the soldier to fake an injury to his head.

When Frederic is introduced to Catherine, both are navigating the transition between the old values and the uncertainty of war. We learn that Catherine's true love was killed in the war and that she shares Frederic's growing disillusionment. Like Agnes, Catherine has known other men and tells Frederic about her fiancé, who was killed in battle. She explains that she joined the war "having the silly idea he might come to the hospital where I was. With a sabre cut, I suppose, and a bandage around his head. Or shot through the shoulder. Something picturesque" but that "he didn't have a sabre cut. They blew him all to bits."[32] She seems emotionally confused and affected by the brutal craziness of the war. When Frederic tries to kiss her, she refuses and slaps him, but, like Agnes, she begins to understand the unpredictability of war and eventually kisses him. Though she once embraced the old values, modern warfare teaches her to live for the moment.

When Frederic leaves for the front, Catherine gives him a Saint Anthony medal. Though the medal was known to protect travelers from harm, Catherine eventually tells him that she doesn't have any religion and that the medal, which he loses, is just for luck. Despite having the medal, like Ernest, Frederic is severely wounded in the right knee and foot on the Italian front. Ernest reflects on his own injury to describe what he experienced, writing:

> My legs felt warm and wet and my shoes were wet and warm inside. I knew that I was hit and leaned over and put my had on my knee. My knee wasn't there. My hand went in and my knee was down on my shin. I wiped my hand on my shirt and another floating light came very slowly down and I looked at my leg and was very afraid. Oh, God, I said get me out of here.[33]

The war experience totally changed Ernest's view of heroism. World War I wasn't his grandfather's war. Being a passive victim in a trench didn't seem heroic to Ernest. When the surgeon Rinaldi visits Frederic in the hospital and praises him for his heroism, Ernest's projects his feelings about war, and Frederic denies any display of heroism:

"Did you do any heroic act?"

"No," I said. "I was blown up while we were eating cheese."[34]

BOOK TWO

Like Ernest, Frederic is moved to a hospital in Milan for better treatment, but Ernest's view of the hospital has changed since his own experience at age nineteen. The hospital is chaotic and unprepared to deal with injured patients The rooms aren't ready, the sheets are locked up, the nurses can't read Frederic's papers written in Italian, and the only doctor is unavailable because he is at Lake Como. Things improve, however, when Miss Gage brings Frederic vermouth and when Catherine arrives. Quickly, Frederic and Catherine feel a strong sense of love and passion. When they make love for the first time, Ernest's fantasies about Agnes are fulfilled:

"I want you, I'm just mad about you."

"You really love me?"

"Don't keep on saying that. Come on. Please. Please, Catherine."

"All right but only for a minute."

"All right," I said. "Shut the door."

"You can't. You shouldn't."

"Come on."

"Don't talk. Please come on."

Ernest uses dialog to describe their love making, then brief description and again more dialogue to convey the lovers' satisfaction:

Catherine sat in a chair by the bed. The door was open into the hall. The wildness was gone and I felt finer than I had ever felt.

She asked, "Now do you believe I love you?"

"Oh, you are lovely," I said. "You've got to stay they can't send you away. I'm crazy in love with you."

"We'll have to be awfully careful. That was just madness. We can't do that."

"We can at night."

"We'll have to be awfully careful. You'll have to be careful in front of other people."

"I will."[35]

The plot of the novel shifts from fantasy to reality and back to fantasy. Like Ernest and Agnes, Frederic and Catherine try to keep their relationship a secret and during the reality of the surgery to remove the bullets from his knee, Frederic is advised not to think about Catherine because the anesthesia will make him blabby. After the surgery, they sit on the balcony and later enjoy horse races and dinners at the galleria.

Like Ernest, Frederic also is attracted to women with beautiful hair. There is an entry in Agnes's diary in which "Mac [another nurse] found one of [Agnes's] yellow hairpins under Ernest's pillow," and Ernest uses and perhaps expands the attraction when Frederic recalls that he:

loved to take her hair down, . . . take out the pins, lay them on the sheet and it would be loose and I would watch her while she kept very still and then take out the last two pins and it would all come down and she would drop her head and we would both be inside of it, and it was the feeling of inside a tent or behind a falls.[36]

Book Two ends when Frederic is called back to the war front, and Catherine informs him that she is three months pregnant.

BOOK THREE

When Frederic returns to the front, the villages have been destroyed, and the morale of the Italian soldiers is low. He realizes that the Italians will not escape if the Austrians attack. In his conversation with Gino, an Italian patriot, Frederic expresses his change in values about the war. Gino believes, "What has been done this summer cannot have been done in vain."[37] Frederic respects Gino's patriotism but doesn't agree with it. Like Ernest, the destruction and loss of life have changed Frederic's belief in heroic action and the values held by his grandfathers. He now is embarrassed by the words "sacred, glorious, and sacrifice and the expression in vain" and "abstract words such as glory, honor, courage, or hallow were obscene beside the concrete names of villages, the numbers of roads, the names of rivers, the numbers of regiments and the dates."[38]

Though Ernest only read about it, the events of the Battle of Caporetto further delineate Ernest's, and Frederic's, disillusionment with war. The Austrians break through the Italian lines, and the Italians retreat. The houses are evacuated, and women and children are loaded in trucks. Ernest describes the retreat as chaotic and emphasizes the horror, confusion, and irrationality of modern warfare. The incompetent Italian soldiers are shooting at their own compatriots. They are frightened and firing at anything they see and are confused because they had heard that there were Germans in Italian uniforms mixing with the retreat in the north.

Frederic reveals his thoughts about the situation:

I did not believe it. That was one of those things you always heard in the war. It was one of the things the enemy always did to you. You did not know any one who went over in German uniform to confuse them. Maybe they did but it sounded difficult. I did not believe the Germans did it. I did not believe they had to. There was no need to confuse our retreat. The size of the army and the fewness of the roads did that. Nobody gave any orders, let alone Germans. Still, they would shoot us for Germans.[39]

As the carabinieri randomly pull Italian officers from the columns of retreating men and execute them on sight, Frederic debates whether he should wait to be questioned or make a break for it. He reasons: "I was obviously a German in Italian uniform. I saw how their minds worked if they had minds and if they worked. They were all young men and they were saving their country."[40]

When Frederic is taken by the military police to the riverbank where officers are being interrogated and executed for the "treachery" that supposedly led to the Italian defeat, Frederic escapes from the senseless cruelty of the carabinieri. He refuses to die for a cause that, to him, seems meaningless, strips himself of the stars that mark him as a lieutenant, and jumps into the river. Afterward, he walks through the plains and jumps aboard a moving train to Milan to find Catherine.

The catastrophic Battle of Caporetto, October–November 1917, was a national disgrace in Italy, and Ernest's humiliating description was so true to history that the Italian government banned the publication of *A Farewell to Arms* from 1929 to 1948, and the illegal 1943 Italian translation prepared by Fernanda Pivano led to her arrest in Turin. The Fascist regime considered the novel detrimental to the honor of the Armed Forces, both in its description of the battle and for the anti-militarism implied in the work.

Ernest's negative depictions of the Italian army were influenced by his personal contempt toward Benito Mussolini. He had interviewed him in 1923, shortly after he seized power, and in an article for the *Toronto Star* called him "the biggest bluff in Europe." Ernest had observed Mussolini trying to impress the media by pretending to be deeply absorbed in reading, while in reality he was holding a French–English dictionary upside down.

Book Four

Reaching Milan, Frederic learns that Catherine has left for Stresa. When Frederic meets Catherine and Helen Ferguson there, their conversation delineates the contrast in values between Fergy and Catherine. Fergy is furious and expresses her traditional values, telling Frederic, "You had a love affair all summer and got this girl with child and now I suppose you'll sneak off."[41] Catherine doesn't feel any need to be married, has accepted her pregnancy, and responds, "We'll both sneak off."[42]

The moral debate continues:

> "You're two of the same thing," Ferguson said. "I'm ashamed of you, Catherine Barkley. You have no shame and no honor and you're as sneaky as he is."
>
> "Don't, Fergy." Catherine said and patted her hand.
>
> "Don't denounce me. You know we like each other."
>
> "Take your hand away," Ferguson said. Her face was red. "If you had any shame it would be different, But you're God knows how many months gone with child and you think it's a joke and are all smiles because your seducer's come back. You've no shame and no feeling."[43]

Though Frederic has been disillusioned by the war, he still has his feet in both moral camps. He is willing to marry Catherine, but she doesn't believe it's important. He has made his separate peace, but feels he is a criminal, a war deserter. He tells Catherine:

> "I feel like a criminal. I've deserted from the army."
>
> "Darling please be sensible. It's not deserting from the army. It's only the Italian army."[44]

When they are informed that Italian police are looking to arrest Frederic, Catherine and Frederic flee to Switzerland.

Book Five

Ernest struggled with the ending of the novel. By his count, he wrote thirty-nine endings before he was satisfied. However, the 2012 edition of the book included forty-seven alternate endings and developed forty-eight possibilities. In the end, Ernest drew on his personal experiences with Hadley, his first wife, to describe the time Federic and Catherine spent together in Switzerland before the birth of their child. Like Ernest and Hadley, Frederic and Catherine live a quiet life in the mountains in a chalet at Les Avants near Montreux.

As the birth of the baby approaches, Frederic and Catherine move to Lausanne to be closer to the hospital, and the tragic end of the story continues to be foreshadowed. The reader learned in Book One that Catherine saw herself dead in the rain. In Book Four, the reader is told, "The world breaks everyone and . . . But those that will not break it kills. It kills the very good and the very gentle and the very brave impartially."[45] In Book Five, the reader learns that the doctor has told Catherine not to drink beer and keep the baby small because she has narrow hips. Then Catherine goes into labor, and Ernest uses his knowledge of childbirth gleaned from his obstetrician father and the near-death birth of his second son, Patrick, who was delivered by Cesarean section to Ernest's second wife, Pauline, to describe the graphic operation.

By the end of the novel, Frederic understands that death is the reality all must face. In many ways, man (and woman) is no better that an ant. He reflects on a camping experience:

> Once in camp I put a log on top of the fire and it was full of ants. As it commenced to burn, the ants swarmed out and went first toward the center where the fire was; then turned back and ran toward the end. When there were enough on the end they fell off into the fire. Some got out, their bodies burnt and flattened, and went off not knowing where they were going. But most of them went toward the fire and then back toward the end and swarmed on the cool end and finally fell off into the fire. I remember thinking at the time that it was the end of the world and a splendid chance to be a messiah and lift the log off the fire and throw it where the ants could get off onto the ground. But I did not do anything but throw a tin cup of water on the log, so that I would have the cup empty to put whiskey in before I added water to it. I think the cup of water on the burning log only steamed the ants.[46]

Frederic now understands that, like Catherine, some die quickly. Others, like him, who survived being blown up in a trench, will be scared but manage to get away. Still others will be unharmed and swarm on to the end of the log until death reaches them. However, in the end death is the fire, which burns us all.

Ernest never forgot the heartbreak and pain of Agnes's infidelity. However, he used his damned hurt as well as his love for her, his physical attraction to her, and the beauty of her personal characteristics to write a bestseller that placed him among the American literary masters. The novel was first serialized in *Scribner's Magazine* in the May 1929 to October 1929 issues. Then the book was published in September 1929 with a first edition print run of approximately thirty-one thousand copies, and Paramount bought the movie rights.

Though the publication of *A Farewell to Arms* made Ernest financially independent, his success was not without controversy. He had dared to write about the good, the bad, and the ugly. His depiction of the Battle at Caporetto showed the disorder and incompetence of the Italian army and the unheroic nature of modern warfare. As a result, his book was banned in Italy and Ernest was publicly derided by Mussolini. Then his depictions of premarital sex were considered pornographic by some, the book was banned in Boston, and many readers of *Scribner's Magazine* cancelled their subscriptions. Yet despite—or maybe because of—its revolutionary content, the book became Ernest's first bestseller and is considered the premier American war novel from World War I.

Hadley

Figure 3.1. Hadley Richardson.
"I knew she was the girl I was going to marry."
Ernest Hemingway Collection. John F. Kennedy Presidential Library and Museum, Boston, Massachusetts.

WHEN THE EXCITEMENT OF THE WAR AND THE EXHILARATION OF LOV-
ing Agnes turned to feelings of isolation and depression, Marcelline
characterized Ernest's return "to conventional, suburban Oak Park living . . . like being put in a box with the cover nailed down."[1] She observed
that despite attention from neighbors and parties with Italian American
clubs, Ernest was depressed. He looked for the mail and seemed on edge
with the waiting. Then, after the letter came and he read it, he went
to bed and was physically ill. She recalled that the family didn't know
what was wrong with him, that he didn't respond to medical treatment,
and that he ran a temperature. When Marcelline confronted him in the
privacy of his bedroom, he simply told her Agnes was not coming to
America and that she was going to marry an Italian major instead. Then
he turned to the wall, was sick for several days, and did not mention the
letter again. Marcelline felt sorry for her brother but later concluded "that
the letter from Agnes may have been the most valuable one my brother
ever received. Perhaps without that rankling memory, *A Farewell to Arms*
might never have been written."[2]

After the war, Ernest suffered both physical and emotional pain. He
rested in the mornings and by lunch put on his Red Cross uniform and
well-polished boots. After lunch with the family, he took his cane and
walked to the high school, a place where he felt at home. However, as
time passed, not having a job became a problem. Marcelline overheard
some high school teachers questioning:

> "Why doesn't he stop trying to be a hero and put on civilian clothes?
> I've got no patience with these kids that keep trying to show off."
> "Maybe he hasn't got any civilian clothes left that fit him."
> "Oh that's not it. He just likes to get the girls crazy about him.
> Have you noticed how he hangs around the high school all the time?
> Wouldn't you think he'd find something else to do? Why doesn't he get
> a job? He likes having the girls moon over him! You know as well as I
> do that's why Ernest Hemingway wears his uniform."[3]

Marcelline quickly defended her brother, saying:

Maybe it would interest you to know why he has to wear that uniform all this time. Pieces of metal keep coming out of his legs. Sometimes he has to wear dressings over the places that are festered. Do you know that those high leather boots give his sore legs support. He doesn't wear those boots for fun, he wears them because he has to. Most people don't know it, but Ernie has a lot of pain. He can't get a job yet as you suggest, because he isn't able to stand on his feet more than a few hours at a time. I don't blame him for hanging around the high school. He just gets darn lonesome, and so would you if you were home and all of your friends were away in college or had jobs during the daytime. I should think teachers like you would be more understanding instead of talking so mean about a boy who's going though all that Ernest to bear![4]

Eventually, Ernest's isolation and depression turned into restlessness. He spent the summer and fall of 1919 in Michigan and the winter of 1920 in Toronto. As a result of a talk he gave to the Ladies Aid Society at the Petoskey Library, he met Mrs. Harriet Connable, who invited Ernest to spend the winter in Toronto as the companion to her disabled son, Ralph Connable Jr., who was one year younger than Ernest. During that winter, Mr. Constable, the head of F. W. Woolworth in Canada, introduced Ernest to his friends at the *Toronto Star*, which led to opportunities for Ernest to write occasional articles for the *Star* until he returned to Oak Park in May 1920.

Ernest planned to spend the summer in Michigan, fishing and relaxing with friends, but the summer of 1920 was filled with family conflict. His father stayed in Oak Park and Ernest was expected to help with chores in Michigan. Ernest did the minimum amount of work but did not meet his family's expectations. He also got into trouble by sneaking away from the cottage for a late-night picnic with his friend, Ted Brumback, his younger sisters, and their teenage girlfriends. Believing that her children were in bed, Grace was shocked and humiliated when the teenage girls' mother confronted Grace at the cottage at 3 a.m. asking where the girls were. Grace's concerns about Ernest's laziness and lack of ambition were reinforced when the woman ended her tirade by telling Grace she should "get rid of those grown men loafing around."[5]

The next morning Ernest and Brumback were told to pack their things and get out of the house. Grace also handed Ernest a letter telling him:

> Unless you, my son Ernest, come to yourself, crease your lazy loafing and pleasure seeking . . . spending all your earnings lavishly and wastefully on luxuries for yourself—stop trading your handsome face to fool little gullible girls, and neglecting your duties to God and Your Savior, Jesus Christ—unless in other words you come into your man hood, there is nothing for you but bankruptcy. *You have overdrawn.*[6]

She further advised him, "do not come back until your tongue has learned not to insult and shame your mother. When you have changed your ideas and aims in life you will find you mother waiting to welcome you, where it be in this world or the next—loving you and longing for your love."[7]

Ernest resented his mother's letter, left the Michigan cottage, and gave up living with his family in Oak Park. Though he told friends, "Having been barred from my domicile I know not where I will linger in Chi," he moved into Kenley and Doodles Smith's Chicago apartment.[8] Kenley was the older brother of Bill and Katy Smith, who lived in St. Louis but spent summers in Horton Bay near the Hemingway cottage.

Life as a boarder at the seven-room apartment was comfortable. Kenley (YK) Smith worked for McCann Erickson and through business connections had access to theater and opera tickets. He was twelve years older than Ernest, well acquainted with writers and painters in Chicago, and took a genuine interest in Ernest's career. Kenley and Doodles loved to entertain and have house guests, and it was at a party at the apartment in late October 1920 that Ernest met Hadley Richardson.

Hadley was born in St. Louis, Missouri, on November 9, 1891. Her father held an executive position at the family drug company, but he died by suicide due to financial worries when Hadley was twelve. Her mother was a domineering woman and a talented pianist with a driving intellectual curiosity. She was very protective of Hadley, who fell from a second story window and suffered a serious back injury when she was two.

Restricted from normal childhood activities, Hadley grew to be painfully shy as an adolescent. She retreated into playing the piano and, after graduation from Mary Institute in St. Louis, entered Bryn Mawr College. However, due to poor health and the firm advice of her mother, she dropped out of college after her freshman year. She continued to study music but did not have the confidence to pursue a serious musical career. Rather, she took care of her mother, who developed Bright's disease, until her mother's death in 1921.

Hadley had no career and was almost thirty when she received an invitation to come to Chicago from Katy Smith, her classmate at Mary Institute, and soon found herself a house guest at the apartment of Kenley and Doodles Smith. When Hadley met the "hulky, bulky something" that turned out to be Ernest, she noted he rarely left her side, but thought he was too dashing and too young to be interested in her.[9] She was wrong. When Ernest saw Hadley, he was immediately attracted to her calm demeanor and her beautiful auburn hair. He told his brother, "The moment she entered the room . . . an intense feeling came over me. I knew she was the girl I was going to marry."[10]

For three weeks, the boarder and the house guest roamed Chicago and had serious conversations. She was twenty-nine and he was only twenty-one, but in many ways, she was the novice and he was the experienced one. While she had played the piano in St. Louis, he had explored the tough sections of Kansas City, survived being wounded in Fossalta, and experienced love in Milan. She was tentative and reserved, and he had boundless energy and belief in the future.

After three weeks in Chicago, Hadley returned to St. Louis then returned to Chicago in early December. Between her visits to Chicago, they corresponded. Hadley's shyness soon dissipated and when Ernest wrote her a "peach" of a letter, she responded in eleven pages. She desperately wanted him to come to St. Louis for New Year's, but he didn't have the financial resources to make the trip. Instead, he sent her an evening bag and she thanked him, saying:

Yes, I think you are the nicest lover a person ever had. . . . I feel snatched up and appreciated and taken care of the way I did the night I rolled

Figure 3.2. Ernest and Hadley, circa 1921.
She was quiet and reserved; he had boundless energy.
Ernest Hemingway Collection. John F. Kennedy Presidential Library and Museum, Boston, Massachusetts.

so fast and scaredly down the sand dunes in the dark and you whirled me up and kissed me—I want to be picked up now . . . if you were here you would be around me and (I would be) domestic and needing to be necessary to. D'you ever feel that way about me? Big and lonely, only, and needing. Huh? Good night Ernest dear, dear. Your Hash.[11]

When Ernest wrote that his Red Cross friend was encouraging him to return to Italy, she told him she would miss him "pretty frightfully," and he responded, saying they should get married and go to Italy together.[12] Her letters emphasized that what was most important to her was his writing and that his ambition must be their guide.

Though Hadley claimed she was "not at all the woman who want(ed) her practical future guaranteed," Ernest pursued his career in writing by getting a job as an editorial assistant for the *Cooperative Commonwealth*, a cooperative movement publication with a circulation of sixty-five thousand with eighty pages of reading matter and about twenty pages of ads.[13]

He immediately reported his employment to his mother, saying "I'm being frightfully good in pursuit of your instructions" and explained "Most of the reading (matter) was written by myself. Also write editorials and most anything. Will write anything once."[14] He then confessed to Bill Smith that his job was not bad except at the end of the month, when he had to "work like hell."[15] He rationalized, "I'm supposed to do a good deal of thinking planning of editorials at home" and explained he went to the office about 9 a.m. and (then took) two or three hours for lunch.[16] After he got a ten dollar raise and was now earning fifty dollars a week, he told his mother, "I am in good shape. I eat well. I sleep well, I do everything but work well."[17]

Though writing for the *Cooperative Commonwealth*, which extolled the benefits of cooperation over the rapacious profiteering of tradesmen, did not meet Ernest's needs as a writer, he still was writing articles for the *Toronto Star*, enjoying Hadley's praise that his "stuff has both rhythm and the right word," and now had the financial ability to visit Hadley in St. Louis.[18]

When he arrived in St. Louis in March 1921, he wore his new Brooks Brothers suit, occasionally paraded around in his Italian cape, and continued his conversations with Hadley about going to Italy together. Hadley wholeheartedly supported the adventure, reasoning, "[Why] wait around and make hoards and piles, instead of working and living along in the way we want and people should—with the person they love."[19] Hadley made it clear to Ernest that neither his age nor his lack of money was important to her. She explained that she had a trust fund from her mother and grandfather that yielded about twenty-five hundred dollars a year and said, "I never expected to find anyone into whose life I could fling my spirit—and now I can—every side of me backs you up."[20] She transferred her own unrealized ambition to be a pianist to support his ambition as a writer, believing "you're honestly the first one that's ever satisfied me intellectually and spiritually."[21] She promised him a Corona typewriter for his birthday; then told him, "I will give you a Corona and you will consequently marry me."[22]

Though she was almost thirty years old and Ernest was barely twenty-two, they looked to one another to define their lives and their futures, and plans for a September wedding commenced. Ernest suggested a church in Horton Bay, Michigan, and Hadley liked the idea. However, Ernest's friends were concerned about the marriage, and Bill Smith tried to talk Ernest out of marrying Hadley because he thought she was too old. Ernest, too, had some moments of nervousness. Feeling the tension that came from giving up his freedom as well as a fishing trip with his Michigan pals, he told Bill Smith, "guy loves a couple or three streams all his life . . . (then) falls in love with a girl and the goddamn stream can dry up for all he cares."[23]

As the wedding approached, Hadley's resolve did not waver. In one of her last letters from St. Louis, she wrote, "I need you in every part of my life. I wanta be kissed I wanta pull your head down on my heart and hold it very close and cradle you there for hours, you blessed thing—love you, love you—your ownest in the world."[24]

When the stirrings of passion once again seized Ernest, his church-going Oak Park morality trumped his need for freedom. On September 3, 1921, Ernest and Hadley were married at the First Presbyterian Church in Horton Bay, Michigan. Thirty guests attended their wedding in the little church decorated with Michigan wildflowers. After a wedding dinner, Ernest rowed his wife across the lake to the family cottage, where they slept on the floor in front of the fireplace on a mattress pulled from one of the beds.

After the Michigan honeymoon, the newlyweds settled into an apartment at 1239 North Dearborn Street in Chicago, and at a dinner with novelist Sherwood Anderson and his wife, they listened to Anderson extoll the advantages of Paris over Italy for Ernest's writing career. Hadley supported a move to Paris, knowing her recent inheritance of eight thousand dollars from her uncle would provide a financial cushion. Then, with Hadley's financial backing and her unwavering faith in his writing, Ernest convinced John Bone, the managing editor of the *Toronto Star*, to agree to publish his dispatches about European events. With letters of introduction from Anderson to Gertrude Stein and Ezra Pound, Ernest and Hadley sailed for France on the French liner *Leopoldina* on December 8, 1921.

Ernest and Hadley soon embraced all Paris had to offer. Paris in the 1920s was a mecca for artists and writers. After the austerity and bloodshed of World War I, pre-war values were rejected and there was much experimentation with new lifestyles, collaborations, and relationships. Expat artists and writers, drawn by the lower cost of living in France, experienced greater acceptance in the European environment than in the prohibition-era United States, and new forms of art and literature thrived. An important ingredient to their experimentation and creativity was collaboration, and Ernest engaged in important connections made in the cafés of the Left Bank and along the Boulevard Montparnasse.

With limited income but much enthusiasm, Ernest and Hadley moved into an apartment at 74 rue du Cardinal Lemoine on the Left Bank near the Place de la Contrescarpe. The fourth-floor walk-up was in a working-class neighborhood and above an all-night dance hall. It contained only two rooms: a living room, where Hadley kept her rented piano, and a bedroom. The kitchen, which was a small attachment to the living room, had a two-burner gas stove. The bathroom consisted of a Turkish toilet located at the bend of the stairs and a bowl, water pitcher, and a slop jar stored in the bedroom closet. The only heat came from the living room fireplace, and any garbage had to be carried down four steep

Figure 3.3. Hadley and Ernest on their wedding day, September 3, 1921, Horton Bay, Michigan.
Marcelline Hemingway Sanford photographs. Ernest Hemingway Foundation of Oak Park Archives, Oak Park Public Library Special Collections, Oak Park, Illinois.

Figure 3.4. Hadley and Ernest with Ernest's sisters, Marcelline and Carol, brother, Leister, and his parents, Grace and Clarence Hemingway, September 3, 1921, Horton Bay, Michigan.

Marcelline Hemingway Sanford photographs. Ernest Hemingway Foundation of Oak Park Archives, Oak Park Public Library Special Collections, Oak Park, Illinois.

Figure 3.5. Ernest and Hadley's Paris apartment, 74 rue Cardinal Lemoine, Paris. "the jolliest place you ever saw."
N. Sindelar Collection.

flights of circular stairs. The rent at 250 francs a month, about eighteen dollars, fit their budget, and Ernest wrote to his parents that the apartment was "the jolliest place you ever saw."[25]

Ernest used his letters of introduction from Sherwood Anderson to meet Gertrude Stein and Ezra Pound, and Ernest and Hadley quickly joined a circle of American writers that included John Dos Passos, Archibald MacLeish, Scott Fitzgerald, and T. S. Eliot. They gathered along with artists like Pablo Picasso and Henri Matisse in the art-filled salon of American expat, art collector, writer, and mentor Gertrude Stein. Their discussions at the salon at 27 rue de Fleurus focused on experimentation and the development of new forms of expression to break free from the past.

Ernest and Hadley loved going to the elegant salon with great paintings:

> It was like one of the best rooms in the finest museum except there was a big fireplace and it was warm and comfortable, and they gave you good things to eat and tea and natural distilled liqueurs made from purple plums, yellow plums or wild raspberries. These were fragrant, colorless alcohols served from cut-glass carafes in small glasses and whether they were quetsche, mirabelle or framboise they all tasted like the fruits they came from, converted into a controlled fire on your tongue that warmed you and loosened it.[26]

They thought "the paintings and the cakes and the eau-de-vie were truly wonderful," appreciated that they were treated as "very good, well-mannered and promising children," and were thrilled when Gertrude and her partner accepted their invitation to tea at their rue du Cardinal Lemoine flat.[27]

Ernest listened with interest to Gertrude's advice on writing, art collecting, and sex. Though he wrote opinionated articles for the *Toronto Star* and worked in a local café on his poetry and short stories, his identity as a writer was not clear, neither to himself nor anyone else. Was he a poet, a short story writer, or a journalist? He worked feverishly at all three genres and was emotionally and financially supported by Hadley, who continued to have total confidence in Ernest as a writer.

However, a jolt to his progress as a writer occurred when his carefully crafted short stories and poems were suddenly lost. When the Lausanne Peace Conference was convened to settle the territorial dispute between Greece and Turkey, Ernest left Paris and went to Lausanne to cover the conference for the *Toronto Star*, and Hadley planned on meeting Ernest in Switzerland. She packed her clothes and, assuming he'd want to work on his writing, she also filled a small suitcase with all of his writing. At the railroad station, she gave her luggage to the porter, but when she got to her compartment the suitcase with Ernest's manuscripts was not there. Together and separately, they furiously searched the train, the railroad stations, the Paris flat, and any number of possible places, but never found the manuscripts nor the carbon copies that also were in the suitcase. Though they slowly accepted the loss, they never forgot it.

They were poor, but they didn't feel poor. Almost always hungry and cold, they relished inexpensive French restaurants and any place that provided warmth. Ernest discovered Sylvia Beach's Shakespeare and Company, a "warm cheerful place with a big stove in winter, tables and shelves of books."[28] When he admitted didn't have enough money to join the rental library, he was grateful that Sylvia said he could pay the deposit any time and still take as many books as he wished. In the evenings, Ernest and Hadley walked along the river and looked in all the galleries and shop windows. They ate at home or in a simple restaurant and then read, went to bed, and made love in the moonlight. Years later, Ernest would sentimentally record the years he spent with Hadley in Paris in his memoir, *A Moveable Feast*, saying, "We ate well and cheaply and drank well and cheaply and slept well and warm together and loved each other."[29]

When Hadley realized she was pregnant, they decided the baby should be born in Toronto, and Ernest returned as a full-time reporter for the *Toronto Star*. Ernest told his sister, "We have a very lovely place here just on the edge of the country across a ravine from the Hunt Club. It is very beautiful, new, light, airy, beautifully and tastefully furnished by ourselves, full of electric fixtures and bath tubs."[30] He added, however,

"We hope not to have to stay here long as we are both homesick for Paris where there are few bathtubs, no electric fixtures, but very nearly all the charm, all the good food and most of the good people in the world."[31] Soon after John Hadley Nicanor Hemingway was born, Ernest quit his job and they moved back to Paris.

The return to Paris defined Ernest as a writer, not a journalist. His ties with the *Toronto Star* were severed, and their only source of income was Hadley's trust fund and whatever compensation Ernest received for reviewing manuscripts for Ford Maddox Ford's *Transatlantic Review*. Their new apartment was above a sawmill at 113 rue Notre-dame-de Champs, but in the Montparnasse neighborhood and the center of intellectual and artistic life of Paris. It was close to Ezra Pound's studio at 70 bis rue Notre-dame-de-Champs, Sylvia Beach's bookstore, and Gertrude Stein's apartment on the rue de Fleurus. Nearby were the Luxembourg Gardens, where they could stroll with their baby.

Gertrude Stein and her partner, Alice B. Toklas, became the baby's godparents. Ernest and Hadley continued to enjoy Stein's large studio filled with Cezannes, Matisses, and Picassos, and Ernest accepted Gertrude's counsel regarding his writing. Stein defined what Ernest had come to think of as the "rotten crowd" as the "Lost Generation." Knowing that this group no longer embraced the values of their elders, the advice of their fathers, or the sayings of their mothers but were forging their way through a new world, they were "lost." The old, pre–World War I values no longer seemed to make sense, and a new set of values or rules by which to live had yet to be clearly defined.

Ernest was fully aware of the change in values and the experimentation with a new way of living that was taking place in Paris. Sex was an open topic for conversation, and homosexual and bisexual relationships were common. In his short stories, he dared to explore subjects considered taboo in Oak Park and questioned values such as marriage, saying in "Three-Day Blow," "Once a man's married, he's absolutely bitched. . . . They get this sort of fat married look. They're done for."[32] Sexual relations and their consequences were also examined. In "Up in Michigan," Ernest detailed the seduction and date rape of Liz Coates, who begins by

Figure 3.6. Hadley and Bumby at home over the sawmill, 113 rue Notre Dame des Champs, Paris, c.1924.

"In Paris, then, you could live very well on almost nothing and by skipping meals occasionally and never buying any new clothes, you could save and have luxuries." *Ernest Hemingway Collection. John F. Kennedy Presidential Library and Museum, Boston, Massachusetts.*

protesting "You mustn't do it, Jim. You mustn't . . . Oh, it isn't right," and ends with "Oh, Jim, Jim. Oh."[33]

Ezra Pound expanded Ernest's literary education by introducing him to James Joyce and T. S. Eliot. These Paris mentors influenced Ernest to let action speak for itself, not tell readers how to respond, eliminate superfluous words, fear abstractions, and use natural symbols that arise organically from the story. Ernest's early short stories reflected his boyhood experiences in Michigan, and in 1923 three hundred copies of *Three Stories and Ten Poems*, containing "Up in Michigan," "Out of Season," and "My Old Man," were published by his new friend Robert McAlmond.

By summer 1924 Bumby was weaned, and Ernest and Hadley went to the Festival of San Fermin in Pamplona. Ernest's hunger for the bullfights was fueled by his fascination with action, ritual, and death. When they returned to Paris from Spain, Ernest was both charged by the physical, emotional, and intellectual qualities of the bullfight and pleased with what he had accomplished after leaving Toronto. He had written ten new stories and all but finished *in our time*. He continued to work on his own writing, the selection and editing of fiction for the *Transatlantic Review*, and broadened his circle of friends to include Scott and Zelda Fitzgerald, Gerald and Sara Murphy, and Pauline Pfeiffer. The winter of 1924–1925 was spent skiing in Schruns, Austria, and another trip to Spain was planned for July 1925.

The 1925 trip to Pamplona included friends and acquaintances that populated the cafés along the Boulevard du Montparnasse. Though Ernest did not accept the mindless behavior of the Montparnasse crowd, he developed an attraction for Lady Duff Twysden, an attractive, twice-divorced English heiress. Being married, Ernest knew he was not free to take up with Duff Twysden but encouraged her flirtatious friendship and whispered conversations. Though Hadley and Ernest appeared to be a happily married couple, Hadley knew Ernest's interest in Duff was not entirely innocent. Yet she maintained an air of cheerful composure. When Ernest was conspicuously absorbed with Duff's flirtations, she went to her room on the pretext that she was tired or had a headache. Believing that husbands were not fair game, Duff stayed out of Ernest's bed due to her personal code and her loyalty to Hadley.

Figure 3.7. Ernest, Hadley, and Bumby in Shruns, Austria, 1925.
Ernest Hemingway Collection. John F. Kennedy Presidential Library and Museum Boston, Massachusetts.

Most of Ernest's friends recognized the infatuation. When Duff flirted with him, he was excited. When she told him that his sexual magnetism tested her self-control, he was elated. When Ernest learned that Duff, who was "engaged" to Pat Guthrie, had spent a romantic weekend with Harold Loeb in St. Jean de Luz, he was visibly jealous. One afternoon after a bullfight there was a scene in which both Ernest and Pat Guthrie began to bait Loeb for his disgust with the brutality of the bullfight. Insults were exchanged. Ernest accused Loeb of "spoiling this party," called him a "lousy bastard," and all but got into a fist fight with him.[34]

Though Ernest's attraction to Duff Twysden probably was never consummated, his jealousy and dislike of Harold Loeb due to his weekend fling with her was immortalized in *The Sun Also Rises*. The Montparnasse crowd who joined Ernest and Hadley on the 1925 trip became the basis for characters in *The Sun Also Rises*. Ernest used his personal experiences and feelings to transform his friends and acquaintances into major characters and created a plot that followed the group of Paris expatriates as they attended the fiesta of San Fermin in Pamplona. Ernest's friends who morphed into major characters are members of the Lost Generation, and their days at the fiesta are filled with mindless drinking, squabbles, and dissipation. Fueled by alcohol, the expatriates wander from bar to bar, fighting senseless battles over women and sex.

The character, Robert Cohn, is based on Harold Loeb, the fellow writer who rivaled Ernest for, and briefly won, the affections of Lady Duff Twysden. Loeb, who came from a wealthy New York family and attended Princeton, is depicted in the novel as having been a champion boxer at Princeton, but one who took up the sport to counteract his Jewish self-consciousness.

Lady Duff Twysden is transformed into Lady Brett Ashley. She is "damned good-looking" and "built with curves like the hull of a racing yacht."[35] Stylish rather than fashionable, she wears jersey sweaters and tweed skirts and brushes her hair back like a boy. Brett is unapologetically sexual, aggressively promiscuous, and actively "turns men into swine."[36] In the novel, Cohn and Brett spend a romantic weekend together, but when Brett pursues other men, Cohn, like Loeb, becomes a lovesick cry-baby, gets into fights, and is the antithesis of grace under pressure. The expatriate crowd mocks and abuses him and often refer to Cohn as a Jew, and once as a "kike."[37] "Take that sad Jewish face away," Brett's jealous fiancé, Mike Campbell, shouts at Cohn. Later, Cohn punches Jake Barnes to the ground and then runs weeping to his room.[38]

Critics have pointed out that Cohn possesses all the traits of a schlemiel, the dreaming, blundering fool from Yiddish folklore. Ernest cleverly uses this stereotype as a foil to grace under pressure by ridiculing Cohn's deviation from the heroic standards of the novel's bullfighters. Cohn is not an easy character to like and is the antithesis of the courageous and stoic code hero, Pedro Romero, but his characterization is vivid and one that tagged Ernest with the accusation of being antisemitic.

Vindictive jealousy colored Ernest's characterizations of Brett Ashley and Robert Cohn. Though the novel was well received by critics, Ernest's friends were not happy when they saw themselves portrayed as self-indulgent, alcoholic, and sexually promiscuous. Duff and Loeb had a romantic interlude in Spain, and Ernest was jealous of Loeb's adventure. He retaliated by giving Loeb cruel fictional immortality in *The Sun Also Rises*. Years after the book was published, Loeb asked Valerie Hemingway, "Why did Ernest do this do me?"[39]

Pauline Pfeiffer also joined Ernest and Hadley's growing circle of friends who attended the festival in Pamplona. Wealthy and chic, she arrived in Paris as the assistant to the Paris editor of *Vogue* magazine and was part of the group Ernest and Hadley called "the rich." Because of her family's money, she could do or buy whatever she wanted. She was slender and more fashionable than Hadley, and, unlike Hadley, was at home with the rich and all the gossip that now fascinated Ernest. As Pauline's feelings for Ernest grew, she believed she would be better for Ernest than Hadley. She read and praised his writing and was prepared to enrich his life financially. She traveled with Ernest and Hadley to Pamplona in 1925, and as winter approached, Ernest agreed to teach her to ski. Maintaining the charade that she was a friend to both Ernest and Hadley, Pauline spent the winter of 1925–1926 with them in Schruns, Austria.

As spring approached, Ernest decided to go to New York to oversee the publication of his next novel, *Torrents of Spring*. Ernest sensed the

Figure 3.8. Ernest Hemingway with friends in Pamplona, Spain, 1925.
L–R: Ernest Hemingway, Harold Loeb (wearing glasses), Lady Duff Twydsen (wearing hat), Hadley Hemingway, Donald Ogden Stewart, Pat Guthrie.
"Why did Ernest do this to me?"
Ernest Hemingway Collection. John F. Kennedy Presidential Library and Museum, Boston, Massachusetts.

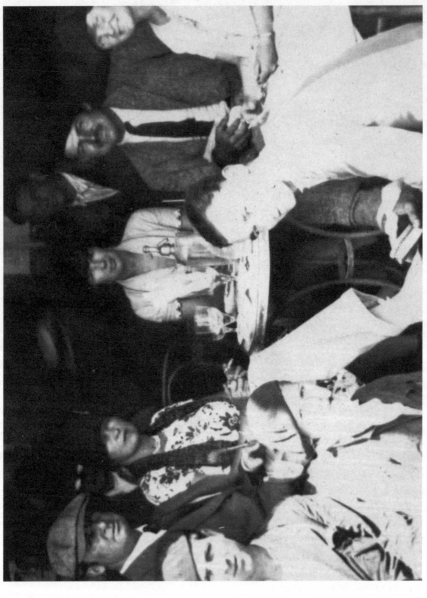

Figure 3.9. Ernest Hemingway with friends, Pamplona, Spain, 1926.
L–R (at table): Gerald Murphy, Sara Murphy, Pauline Pfeiffer, Ernest and Hadley Hemingway.
Ernest Hemingway Collection. John F. Kennedy Presidential Library and Museum, Boston, Massachusetts.

potential success of *The Sun Also Rises* and worked to break his contract with the American publisher Boni & Liveright by writing *Torrents of Spring*. In doing so, he satirized the work of Sherwood Anderson, a popular Boni & Liveright author, so that Boni & Liveright would refuse to publish *Torrents*, and he would then be free to send the manuscript of *The Sun Also Rises* to Max Perkins at Scribner's. While Hadley did not support Ernest's use of their longtime friend, Sherwood Anderson, to further his publication interests, Pauline Pfeiffer did.

That spring, Pauline went to Paris to cover the new designer collections for *Vogue*, and Hadley and Bumby stayed in Schruns. Pauline wrote numerous letters to her "friend," Hadley, but also urged Ernest to stop in Paris on his way to New York. After Ernest left Paris for New York, Pauline wrote to Hadley saying, "your husband, Ernest, was a delight to me. I tried to see him as much as he would see me and was possible."[40] When Ernest returned from New York, he stopped again in Paris to see Pauline. Though he intended to return to Schruns and Hadley and Bumby, he stayed in Paris with Pauline. He later recalled, "I should have caught the first train from the Gare de l'Est that would take me down to Austria. But the girl I was in love with was in Paris then, and I did not take the first train, or the second or the third."[41]

Ernest's attraction to Duff Twysden had been obvious to many, but now he was entangled in the complexities of serious infidelity. When Ernest was with Pauline, he felt "unbelievable wrenching, killing happiness," but he also knew he was being selfish and the "treachery of everything" gave him feelings of "terrible remorse."[42] Naively, what he wanted was to have both Hadley and Pauline; he wasn't ready to give up either one. Pauline was persistent and maintained her presence either by continuing to travel with Ernest and Hadley or by a barrage of letters sent to both of them. When Hadley started to ask questions regarding Ernest's interest in Pauline, Ernest resented her forcing the issue. For a while, Hadley tried to go on as before, but eventually, she gave Ernest a choice. She said if he and Pauline would separate for one hundred days, and then still wanted to be together after the separation, she would consent to a divorce. In less than one hundred days, however, Hadley recognized her marriage to Ernest was over, filed for divorce, and moved with Bumby to an apartment at 35 rue des Fleurus near Gertrude Stein and Alice B. Toklas's salon.

Ernest later characterized Pauline's friendship with Hadley as the "oldest trick there is."[43] However, he thrived on excitement and emotional highs and at the time could not withdraw from his affair with Pauline. As his career advanced, so did his tendencies to pursue a life of physical and emotional risk. Along with Hadley's emotional and financial encouragement, he had reaped rewards for leaving his Midwest home and branching out to meet new people and see new places. Now, again, he was feeling that hunger, if not addiction, for the intensity and freedom that came from leaving "home," wherever that home or place might be. Ernest moved on to new places, new people, and new adventures. However, he would always harbor feelings of guilt and remorse for leaving Hadley and Bumby. Thirty years and three marriages later, he would use his memories and experiences from the years he spent with Hadley in Paris to create his memoir, *A Moveable Feast*.

In November 1956, while having lunch at the Ritz Hotel in Paris, Ernest recovered two small steamer trunks that he had stored in the hotel's basement in March 1928. The trunks contained notebooks he had filled during the 1920s. Using his personal accounts to create his memoir, he recalled the kindness of Sylvia Beach; the influences of Ezra Pound, F. Scott Fitzgerld, and Gertrude Stein; and the warm, loving relationship he shared with Hadley. The memoir was published posthumously in 1964, three years after Ernest's death, by Mary Hemingway, his fourth wife and widow, based on his original manuscripts and notes. While some critics claim Mary deleted Ernest's lengthy apology to Hadley because it impugned her own role as his wife, there are numerous passages that reflect his lasting love for Hadley.

Though he was a willing participant in his affair with Pauline, he later viewed himself as victim of Pauline's skill in using the "oldest trick," saying:

> we had been infiltrated by [a] rich using the oldest trick there is. It is that an unmarried young woman becomes the temporary best friend of another young woman who is married, goes to live with the husband and wife and she unknowingly, innocently and unrelentingly sets out to

Figure 3.10. Hadley, "Voralberg boy" (Bumby), and Ernest in Schruns, Austria, spring 1926.
"I wish I had died before I loved anyone but her."
Ernest Hemingway Collection. John F. Kennedy Presidential Library and Museum, Boston, Massachusetts.

marry the husband. When the husband is a writer and doing difficult work so that he is occupied much of the time and is not a good companion or partner to his wife for a big part of the day, the arrangement has advantages until you know how it works out. The husband has two attractive girls around when he has finished work. One is new and strange and if he has bad luck he gets to love them both.[44]

He also shows Hadley's unwavering love and loyalty and his own love for her even after he's been in Paris with another woman. Returning to Schruns from Paris by train, he says:

> When I saw my wife again standing by the tracks as the train came in by the piled logs at the station, I wished I had died before I ever loved anyone but her. She was smiling, the sun on her lovely face tanned by the snow and sun, beautifully built, her hair red gold in the sun, grown out all winter awkwardly and beautifully, and Mr. Bumby standing with her, blond and chunky and with winter cheeks looking like a good Voralberg boy.
>
> "Oh Tatie," she said, when I was holding her in my arms, "you're back and you made such a fine successful trip. I love you and we've missed you so."
>
> I loved her and I loved no one else and we had a lovely magic time while we were alone. I worked well and we made great trips, and I thought we were invulnerable again, and wasn't until we were out of the mountains in late spring, and back in Paris that the other thing started again.[45]

Ernest eventually left Paris and continued his lifelong adventure but knew that Paris would never be the same again. He wistfully concludes his memoir saying, "this is how Paris was when we were very poor and very happy."[46]

Pauline

Figure 4.1. Pauline Pfeiffer.
"She used the oldest trick."
Apic/Getty Images

PAULINE WAS YOUNGER, THINNER, AND MORE STYLISH THAN HADLEY, but she, too, was utterly devoted to Ernest Hemingway, the writer. Determined to be with Ernest, she had followed Hadley and Ernest to Austria, Spain, and later France. She caught his attention and fed his ego by listening to the latest draft chapters of *Torrents of Spring* and was one of the few people who supported its publication. She liked to think that their mutual interest in writing made them soulmates and was committed to providing a lifestyle that nurtured Ernest's career as a writer.

A graduate of University of Missouri's School of Journalism, Pauline first worked on the night desk at the *Cleveland Star*. Then her career path took her to New York and *Vanity Fair*, whose publisher then reassigned her to Paris, where she covered fashion shows for *Vogue*. Like Hadley, Pauline came from St. Louis, but her family was more successful financially, and her trust fund was larger than Hadley's. Her father had developed a chain of drug stores in Missouri and then purchased sixty thousand acres of lucrative Arkansas farmland, while her adoring Uncle Gus held controlling stock in Warner Pharmaceuticals and Richard Hudnut Cosmetics. Her mother raised Pauline as a devout Catholic and sent Pauline and her sister to Catholic girls' schools before going on to college.

Though it was popular and very French to have a wife at home and a mistress on the side, this type of arrangement wasn't going to work for Pauline. She was a practicing Catholic, believed that extramarital sex was a sin, and had reservations about contraception. Since the threat of pregnancy also was a concern, marriage within the Catholic Church was required.

Though Ernest no longer embraced the Protestantism of his parents, he had considered conversion to Catholicism. On January 2, 1926, Ernest had written to Ernest Walsh, saying "If I am anything I am a Catholic. Had extreme unction administered to me as such in July 1918 and recovered. So guess I am a super-catholic. . . . Am not what is called a 'good' catholic. . . . But cannot imagine taking any other religion seriously."[1]

In order to marry Pauline, Ernest used the extreme unction given to him after he was injured in Italy as the basis for declaring that he was a Catholic. Since Hadley was not Catholic, the conversion annulled his marriage to her and allowed his marriage to Pauline. The results of the April 25, 1927, canonical inquest into Ernest's standing in the Catholic Church by the Archdiocese of Paris confirmed and reported that he was "certified a Catholic in good standing."[2]

After Ernest and Hadley's divorce was final on April 14, 1927, Ernest married Pauline on May 10, 1927, in a Catholic ceremony at L'Eglise de St. Honore-d'Eylau on the place Victor Hugo in Paris. Ernest wore a three-piece suit and Pauline a silk dress and a single strand of pearls. Pauline's sister, Jinny, witnessed the ceremony and a few close friends gathered afterword for a wedding luncheon. Ernest and Pauline's parents were not present, but cables, letters, and checks soon arrived from across the Atlantic.

Ernest and Pauline moved into an antique-filled apartment at 6 rue Ferou near the Luxembourg Gardens. Pauline selected an apartment that had a salon, dining room, full kitchen, large bedroom, a maid's room, two bathrooms, and a study, where Ernest could write. Given his new surroundings and Pauline's influence, Ernest ordered new suits from a rue St. Honore tailor, had them properly fitted, and began working on his next novel, *A Farewell to Arms*, now in the comfort of his own study.

In less than a year, Pauline was pregnant, and they decided it was time to go back to the United States. In March 1928, Ernest and Pauline sailed on the *Orita* from La Rochelle, France, to Havana, Cuba, and from there took a ferry to Key West, Florida. Ernest's Key West attraction was fueled by John Dos Passos's stories of hitch-hiking through the tropical island that stretched into the Caribbean from the Florida peninsula. The six weeks Ernest and Pauline intended to spend in Key West turned into twelve years. The years in Key West were fertile ones. There he wrote *A Farewell to Arms* (1929), *Death in the Afternoon* (1932), *Green Hills of Africa* (1935), and *To Have and Have Not* (1937), and began *For Whom the Bell Tolls*. In Paris, Ernest had found his voice by learning to write about his experiences. In Key West, he tried to master it.

Still handsome, but now successful and even more confident, Ernest made friends easily. They were not the literary influences that nurtured his talent in Paris, but rather a mix of fishermen, millionaires, and colorful characters he met on the docks and in the bars. Bahamian-born

Figure 4.2. Ernest and Pauline Hemingway's wedding photo, Paris, 1927.
*Ernest Hemingway Collection. John F. Kennedy Presidential Library and
Museum, Boston, Massachusetts.*

Bra Saunders taught Ernest deep-sea fishing; Joe Russell, owner of
Sloppy Joe's Bar and a Prohibition rum smuggler, became a loyal fishing
companion; while Charles Thompson, whose wealth was derived from
marine hardware and a fleet of fishing vessels, eventually became his
African safari companion. Very quickly, Ernest fell into a routine. There
was intense work during the early morning hours, life on the water in the
afternoons, and, at sundown, talking with sailors, fishermen, and Cuban
millionaires at the long, front-to-rear bar at Sloppy Joe's. The handsome
writer with an engaging smile and growing fame quickly made Key West
his new home.

Figure 4.3. Ernest and Pauline Hemingway's Paris apartment, 6 rue Ferou, Paris. *N. Sindelar Collection.*

Calling Key West "the best place I've ever been any time anywhere," Ernest encouraged his family and closest friends to join him and Pauline on the exotic, tropical island he found so conducive to work and play.[3] French-speaking Bumby arrived from Paris, as well as Gerald and Sara Murphy, Archibald and Ada MacLeish, and John and Katy Dos Passos. Perhaps more surprising was a visit from Clarence and Grace Hemingway, who also were in Florida to check on their real estate investments. Clarence was in poor health and worried about his real estate investments, but there were discussions and later an exchange of letters regarding where the new baby should be delivered. Ernest wrote to his father about the prospects of the baby being born in Michigan. Clarence advised against it but offered "his services" to attend Pauline at Oak Park

Hospital. In the end, Patrick Hemingway was delivered after eighteen hours of labor by Caesarian section in Kansas City on June 28, 1928.

Ernest and Pauline had a healthy, nine-and-a-half-pound son, but the delivery was life-threatening, and the doctor warned Pauline that unless she wanted to become a corpse, she shouldn't become pregnant for at least three years. Ernest described the harrowing delivery experience metaphorically, saying, "They finally had to open Pauline up like a picador's horse to lift out Patrick. It is a different feeling seeing the *tripas* (Spanish for guts) of a friend rather than those of a horse to whom you have never been introduced."[4] Given his habit of writing about his experiences, he used Pauline's ordeal to craft the graphic description of Catherine's Caesarian section at the end of *A Farewell to Arms*.

After leaving the hospital, Pauline convalesced in at her parents' home in Pigott, Arkansas, but as soon as the baby was christened, she left the baby with her sister and joined Ernest in Wyoming. Pauline was more interested in being a wife than a mother, and Ernest had gone to Wyoming in search of cool weather, good fishing, and the opportunity to finish *A Farewell to Arms*. When Ernest wasn't writing, they shot sharp-tailed grouse or fished for trout. At the end of August, they headed across the country on the thousand-mile journey back to Arkansas in a car purchased for them by Pauline's Uncle Gus.

Though Ernest tried to maintain his rituals of writing, there were many distractions—a new baby, the travel back and forth to Wyoming, a visit by Bumby, and then on December 6, 1928, the suicide of his father. Worried about family finances due to the Florida real estate investments as well as his deteriorating health due to diabetes, Clarence shot himself in the head in the master bedroom of the home on Kenilworth Avenue with his father, Anson's, Smith & Wesson revolver.

Upon receiving the news of his father's death, Ernest borrowed money from Scott Fitzgerald and immediately went to Oak Park. After the funeral he wrote to Max Perkins, saying:

> My father shot himself—I was very fond of him and feel like hell about it. Got to Oak Park in plenty of time to handle things. . . . Have every-thing fixed up except they will have damned little money.—Realize of

course that thing for me to do is not worry but get to work—finish my book properly so I can help them out with the proceeds—there are my Mother and two kids boy 12 and girl 16 still at home—$25,000 insurance—$15,000 mortgage on the house—Various worthless land in Michigan, Florida etc. with taxes on all of it. No other capital—all gone—My father carried 20–30 year endowment insurance which was paid and lost in Florida.—Sunk all his savings, my grandfather's estate etc., in Florida.[5]

However, despite the grim financial circumstances, Ernest reassured his mother, saying, "Never worry because I will always fix things up—can always borrow money—if I haven't it. So don't ever worry but go ahead with good confidence and get things going. . . . Remember you are on your own but have a powerful backer—To whit me."[6]

Then in anticipation of the Kenilworth Avenue house being sold, Ernest asked his mother for Anson's .32 caliber Smith & Wesson "Long John" Civil War revolver, the suicide gun, and she sent it to him. He also requested his mother to put "my [war] trophies . . . in a trunk or box and store them if you sell the house as I value them very much for Bumby."[7]

Despite his supportive letter to his mother, Ernest was worried about finances. He and Hadley had lived frugally, but now Ernest was a conspicuous figure and married to a woman who preferred to subsidize their lifestyle rather than sacrifice any accustomed comforts. At the time of his father's death, Ernest had been working on his next novel rather than writing and getting paid for short stories or magazine articles and had to borrow one hundred dollars from Scott Fitzgerald for his train ticket to Chicago. His risk-taking father had put all the family's savings into Florida land and had not paid attention to bills due to his illness. Ernest now felt responsible for supporting a wife, a mother, two sisters, a brother, ex-wife, two sons, and three servants. Though he tended to exaggerate the number of people dependent on him and the extent of his expenses, he hoped that profits from *A Farewell to Arms* would be enough to support his new lifestyle and a trust fund for this mother.

The success of *A Farewell to Arms* placed Ernest among the American literary masters. Max Perkins, Ernest's editor at Scriber's, summarized the reviews as "splendid," and Ernest received the praise he had longed for when his mother wrote, "It is the best you have done yet—and deserves the high praise it is receiving."[8] Scribner's paid Ernest sixteen thousand dollars to serialize the work, the initial printing of over thirty-one thousand copies sold immediately, and Paramount bought the movie rights. Ernest put most of his earnings, thirty thousand dollars, into a trust fund for his mother, and Pauline and Uncle Gus contributed another twenty thousand dollars.

Following the publication of *A Farewell to Arms* and the suicide of his father, Ernest wanted to travel back to Spain to study the bullfights. He had experienced violence and death in his own life and had come to understand, "All stories, if continued long enough, end in death."[9] Now he decided to explore the feelings and attitudes associated with facing death. He claimed he wanted to go to Spain to make sense of death, to write a non-fiction work that detailed a matador's skill in playing with death and explain his belief that bullfighting was not just a sport, but rather a drama that combined athleticism with artistry.

In his book, *Death in the Afternoon*, Ernest explains that this dangerous artform known as a bull fight is created by the matador's ability to dare a bull to come closer and closer in the course of the fight. Emotion is given to the viewer by the closeness with which the matador brings the bull past his body, and it is prolonged by the slowness with which he can execute the pass. As the drama unfolds, "He (the matador) gives the feeling of his immortality, and, as you watch it, it becomes yours."[10]

Death in the Afternoon reflects Ernest's fascination with and commitment to understanding how men face death. Filled with vivid description, the book is a scholarly treatise on the art of bullfighting. Though the book's dedication reads, "To Pauline," and Pauline left Patrick with a nurse in order to be with Ernest in Spain, her presence is not reflected in the story. Rather, when interjecting the topic of love, only the lingering pain of leaving Hadley appears, as he seems compelled to comment, "I would sooner have the pox than to fall in love with another woman loving the one I have."[11]

After Ernest completed the research and initial drafts of the book, Ernest and Pauline returned to America aboard the *Ile de France* in

September 1931. Ernest planned to finish his book in Key West, and Pauline planned to prepare for the birth of their second child in November. However, on their return from Spain aboard the *Ile de France*, Ernest and Pauline met Jane Mason, wife of Grant Mason, a wealthy Yale graduate and head of Pan American Airways for the Caribbean. Jane was twenty-two, strawberry blonde, and, unlike Pauline, who was seven months pregnant at the time, danced and drank with great enthusiasm. By the time they reached New York, Jane was a friend to both Pauline and Ernest. Initially, Pauline was not threatened by Jane, but Ernest now was attracted to a new woman who enjoyed deep-sea fishing and pigeon shooting, had a wide circle of wealthy friends, and had an adventurous personality streak.

On November 11, 1931, Pauline gave birth to Gregory Hancock Hemingway in Kansas City by Caesarean section after a twelve-hour labor, and on September 23, 1932, *Death in the Afternoon* was published. The baby was a healthy nine-pound boy with big feet. The book received mixed reviews as the focus was on a blood sport many readers found disgusting or of little interest.

After returning to Key West, Ernest was restless. Disappointed with the reviews of *Death in the Afternoon*, he bought a boat and began spending more and more time on the water. Cuba was only ninety miles from Key West, surrounded by waters abundant with fish and populated by people and a culture that was warm and friendly. Having met Grant and Jane Mason on board the *Ile de France*, Ernest began spending time with Jane Mason, who lived at Jaimanitas, a grand estate thirty minutes west of Havana.

At first, they were just friends. They fished on board Joe Russell's *Anita* or Ernest's thirty-eight-foot cabin cruiser, *Pilar*, or shot pigeons at Club de Cazadores. A beautiful, accomplished sportswoman, Jane was easily drawn to Ernest and saw him freely, without her husband. While Jane occasionally visited Ernest and Pauline in Key West, bringing live flamingos and other exotic house gifts, Ernest started to spend months at a time in Cuba.

Though deceiving Hadley left Ernest bruised and remorseful, he rationalized a new infidelity, believing that his sexual relations with

Figure 4.4. Carlos Gutierrez and Jane Mason aboard "Sloppy Joe" Russell's *Anita*. *Ernest Hemingway Collection. John F. Kennedy Presidential Library and Museum, Boston, Massachusetts.*

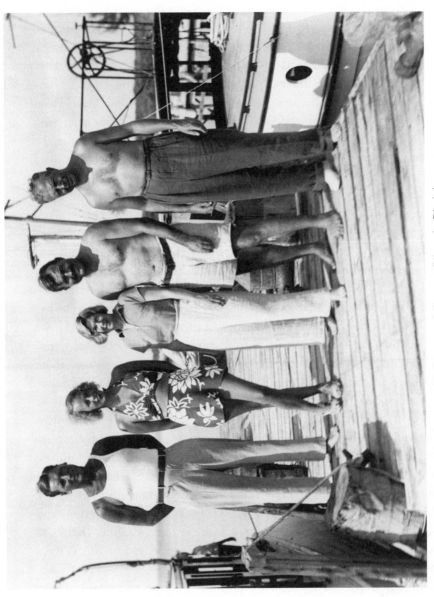

Figure 4.5. Ernest and Pauline Hemingway with Baron and Eva von Blixen in Bimini. Pauline bleached her hair and told Ernest, "I think you'll like me."

Ernest Hemingway Collection. John F. Kennedy Presidential Library and Museum, Boston, Massachusetts.

Pauline were not satisfying. Accepting the strict admonition of her Kansas City obstetrician that she not become pregnant for a third time, Ernest claimed it was necessary to practice coitus interruptus, since other forms of birth control were prohibited by Pauline's Catholicism. Sexual coolness set in, and Ernest, not Pauline, now initiated long separations. Though Pauline would visit Havana for two- or three-week periods, mostly she was at home in Key West, and Room 511 in the Ambos Mundos Hotel in Havana became yet another new home for Ernest. From Havana, Ernest fished in the Gulf Stream and wrote a series of articles for *Esquire*. In "A Cuban Letter," he recounted the magic of leaving the harbor in the early morning, describing the pleasure of lunches cooked over an open fire on a deserted beach, and the thrill of catching a 750-pound marlin, but he never told his readers that the days on the water and nights in Havana were shared with Jane Mason.

From Key West, Pauline began the practice of trying to lure Ernest back home. She wrote, "I miss you very much and all the time and will follow you around like a little dog and so will Patrick. Gregory looks too swell with his four teeth and his silky, curly hair. . . . Hurry, hurry, hurry, can't, wait any longer than is possible."[12] Then making reference to her new hair style and blonde color, she says, "I think you'll like me."[13] However, despite the attractions of Patrick, now three, the new baby, and Pauline's attempts to make herself more attractive, Ernest engaged in an affair with Jane and began to refer to Pauline as POM, Poor Old Mama.

Pauline had learned to endure life-threatening childbirth, the tedious aspects of motherhood, and life in a subtropical "paradise" filled with small, rundown houses and salty, if not unsavory, sailors and fishermen. Now with two children and her perceived need for servants and nurses, living in a rented apartment was no longer acceptable. She looked for and found a house that could be renovated as a suitable home for her family. Her Uncle Gus negotiated the purchase, provided the eight thousand dollars in cash, and had the title made to Ernest and Pauline. Thanks to Uncle Gus, Ernest, Pauline, Patrick, and Gregory moved to 907 Whitehead Street in December 1931.

Built in 1851, the Spanish Colonial-style house had wrought-iron railings encircling both the first and second floors, high ceilings, and

Figure 4.6. Ernest Hemingway and Pauline Pfeiffer's house, 907 Whitehead Street, Key West, Florida, purchased by Pauline's uncle, Gus Pfeiffer, for Pauline and Ernest.
Ernest Hemingway Collection. John F. Kennedy Presidential Library and Museum, Boston, Massachusetts.

shuttered windows. Almost every room looked out on the lush garden filled with fig, banyan, and lime trees. Built long before the days of air conditioning, the high ceilings and vertically aligned windows helped to keep the house cool. Because Key West did not have access to fresh water until 1941, the metal roof enabled the collection of rainwater, which was stored in a cistern. The ground floor contained a spacious living room, dining room, and kitchen. Upstairs there were bedrooms, and the carriage house was to be transformed into a library and study for Ernest.

Figure 4.7. Ernest's study above the carriage house, Key West, Florida.
N. Sindelar Collection.

While Ernest was away, Pauline oversaw renovations to the house. She added crystal chandeliers to the living room, dining room, and master bedroom; enhanced the walkways with decorative tiles; and had her furniture shipped from Paris. The carriage house became a quiet retreat for writing, away from the activity of the main house, and was accessed by a catwalk. The walls of the study were lined with bookshelves, and the room was furnished with a round table, a leather-covered cigar factory stick chair, a typewriter, and eventually hunting trophies.

Meanwhile, rumors began to circulate that Jane entered Ernest's room at the Ambos Mundos by climbing through a fifth-floor transom window and was becoming a danger to herself and others due to driving her oversized Packard at breakneck speeds on the narrow, curving roads of Cuba. When her mercurial temperament led to her attraction to other men and stories about her need for psychoanalysis due to a failed suicide attempt, Ernest's interest in Jane cooled, and he began planning a trip to Africa.

For a long time, Ernest had talked of a safari in Africa, and Pauline fully supported the trip. She understood that the beautiful and adventurous socialite was more interested in a "friendship" with Ernest than her and hoped that Ernest's interests and energies would be diverted away from Jane Mason and Cuba and toward the execution of a new adventure. Her instincts were right. Ernest's safari planning included purchasing a high-powered, custom-made Springfield rifle with a telescope; watching a rehearsal of lion tamer, Clyde Beatty, to study the crouching and springing action of lions; and engaging Philip Percival, who had hunted with Winston Churchill and Teddy Roosevelt, as a guide.

On August 7, 1933, Ernest, Pauline, and Charles Thompson left for East Africa with Uncle Gus underwriting the twenty-five-thousand-dollar adventure for Ernest and Pauline. Traveling across the Serengeti Plain under the snow-capped Mt. Kilimanjaro, Ernest shot four lions, two leopards, thirty-five hyenas, as well as a number of cheetahs, a roan antelope, and numerous gazelles. The planning paid off as the prizes of the trip included not only the hunting trophies, but also a set of impressions and experiences (including amebic dysentery) that were recorded in articles sent back to *Esquire* and in the pages of *The Green Hills of*

Figure 4.8. Ernest Hemingway posing with a rhinoceros and African boy, safari in Africa, 1933–1934.
Ernest Hemingway Collection. John F. Kennedy Presidential Library and Museum, Boston, Massachusetts.

Africa, "The Short Happy Life of Francis Macomber" and "The Snows of Kilimanjaro."

As usual, Ernest wrote from experience. The *Esquire* articles promoted Hemingway, the legendary sportsman, who chronicled the quality and quantity of the African game and recorded for his American readers the herds of animals migrating across the Serengeti Plain along with the companion populations of hyenas and vultures. *The Green Hills of Africa* also focused on the experiences of the trip and described the beauty of the African landscape and the action of big game hunting in a non-fiction form. In the foreword, Ernest warned his readers:

Figure 4.9. Ernest Hemingway posing with a lion, safari in Africa, 1933–1934. *Ernest Hemingway Collection. John F. Kennedy Presidential Library and Museum, Boston, Massachusetts.*

> Unlike many novels, none of the characters or incidents in this book is imaginary. Any one not finding sufficient love interest is at liberty, while reading it, to insert whatever love interest he or she may have at the time. The writer has attempted to write an absolutely true book to see whether the shape of a country and the pattern of a month's action can, if truly presented, compete with a work of the imagination.[14]

Though much of the narrative describes Ernest's hunting adventures, his comments about literature and authors are also interspersed. According to Ernest, "The good writers are Henry James, Stephen Crane, and Mark Twain . . . [and] All modern American literature comes from one book by Mark Twain called *Huckleberry Finn*. . . . it's the best book we've had. . . . There was nothing before. There has been nothing as good since."[15]

The Green Hills of Africa initially was serialized in *Scribner's Magazine* and then was published in October 1935 to a first edition print run of 10,500 copies. The reviews were mixed. *New York Times* critic C. G. Poore hailed *The Green Hills of Africa* as "the best-written story of big-game hunting anywhere,"[16] but critic John Chamberlain claimed, "Mr. Hemingway has so simplified his method that all his characters talk the lingo perfected in *The Sun Also Rises*, whether these characters are British, Austrian, Arabian, Ethiopian or Kikuyu."[17]

The criticism of the book sent Ernest into a deep depression. Worried about his decline as a writer, he said he was "ready to blow my lousy head off,"[18] but within a few months he started to blame his perceived decline on the corrupting influence of the wealthy women in his life, his wife, Pauline, and his mistress, Jane Mason. This time he used his hurt, and now his bitterness, to write two short stories set in Africa. Both featured husbands married to wealthy domineering women and reveal Ernest's fears regarding the negative influences of associating with the rich and his insecurities about his future as a writer.

"The Short Happy Life of Francis Macomber" is set in Africa, where a married couple, Francis and Margaret (Margot) Macomber, are on safari, accompanied by Robert Wilson, an English professional hunter and guide. The reader learns that earlier Francis had shot a lion but did not kill it. When Francis and the guide approached the injured lion, the lion charged and "The next thing he (Francis) knew he was running; running wildly, in panic in the open, running toward the stream."[19] As they return to their camp, the wife, Margot, mocks Francis for his cowardice in running from the charging lion. She kisses Wilson, the guide, on his mouth and later further humiliates Francis by sleeping with Wilson, knowing that her husband, as with past infidelities, will do nothing about it. In a heated exchange, Francis says, "You think I will take anything." "I know you will," she replies.[20]

At breakfast the next morning, Wilson can tell that Francis knows what has happened, but he doesn't show any remorse. Though Wilson sleeps with Margot, he is no admirer of rich American women. Based on his previous guiding expeditions, he knows women like Margot:

> are the hardest in the world; the hardest, the cruelest, the most predatory and the most attractive and their men have softened or gone to pieces nervously as they have hardened. Or is it that they pick men they can handle? They can't know that much at the age they marry, he thought. He was grateful that he had gone through his education on American women before now because this was a very attractive one.[21]

After breakfast, the three of them go out to hunt buffalo. Francis is so filled with rage and humiliation that he forgets his fear and kills the biggest buffalo that crosses their path. He also kills another, which Wilson has brought down but only wounded. Buoyed by his success, Francis starts to behave differently, and Margot is unnerved by his change. Francis and the guide, Wilson, pursue the wounded buffalo, and Francis prepares to shoot the charging buffalo, but as the buffalo charges toward Francis, the reader learns, "Mrs. Macomber . . . had shot at the buffalo with the 6.5 Mannlicher as it seemed about to gore Macomber and had hit her husband about two inches up and little to one side of the base of this skull."[22] However, the reader is left wondering whether she was trying to save her husband by aiming for the charging buffalo that was attacking her husband or whether, as Wilson believes, she deliberately aimed her shot Francis, knowing he had become assertive and that she had lost control of him.

In the story, Ernest explores the emasculation of a man married to a beautiful, wealthy, and controlling woman, one that is "simply enameled in that American female cruelty [one of] . . . the damnedest women. Really the damnedest."[23] He considers, "How should a woman act when she discovers her husband is a bloody coward? She's damn cruel but they're all cruel. . . . They govern, of course, and to govern one has to be cruel sometimes. Still, I've seen enough of their damn terrorism."[24]

Neither Francis nor Margot are likeable characters, but they are real. They are characters based on Ernest's experiences with "the rich" he met while married to Pauline. Francis Macomber, an accomplished hunter, holds a number of big-game fishing records, but he does not have the respect of his wife. He is a trust fund man, who "was wealthy and would become wealthier" and hangs on to his money and to his wife "with a great tolerance which seemed the nice thing about him if it were not the most sinister."[25]

Margot is modeled after Jane Mason, beautiful but unfaithful. Like Jane, who had posed for cosmetic ads, Margot is "an extremely handsome and well-kept woman of the beauty and social position which had, five years before, commanded five thousand dollars as the price for endorsing, with photographs, a beauty product which she had never used."[26] Ernest, like Wilson, was intrigued by Jane's beauty, but eventually put off by her wealth and reckless behavior. Ernest claimed that "when I first knew her (Jane) she'd been lovely," but later said that Margot Macomber had been invented "complete with handles from the worst bitch I knew. . . . Not my dish, not my pigeon, not my cup of tea, but lovely for what she was and I was her all of the above which is whatever you make of it. This is as close as I can put it and keep it clean."[27]

Ernest portrays the marriage of Francis and Margot as one of demeaning convenience. Living in Key West, Ernest had come to understand and participate in "white mischief." He modeled Francis after Grant Mason, who understood the adulterous attraction between Ernest and Jane, but accepted a marriage of "demeaning convenience" and continued to maintain a facade of status quo believing it was the civilized thing to do. Like Grant Mason, Francis passively accepts his wife's infidelities. "They were known as a comparatively happily married couple, one of those whose disruption is often rumored but never occurs."[28] "Margot was too beautiful for Macomber to divorce her and Macomber had too much money for Margot ever to leave him."[29] The reader is left with an ambiguous ending, but when asked Ernest said:

> I don't know whether she shot him on purpose any more than you do. I could find out if I asked myself because I invented it and I could go right on inventing . . . the only hint I could give you is that it is my belief that the incidence of husbands shot accidentally by wives who are bitches and really work at it is very low.[30]

Similarly, "The Snows of Kilimanjaro" is also set in Africa and focuses on two wealthy people trapped in an unhappy marriage. It also reveals Ernest's concern about the impact the rich have on his writing and his nervousness about his own decline as a writer. The character, Harry, is a writer, dying of gangrene, and his wealthy and once beautiful and sexually attractive wife, Helen, becomes the victim of his caustic comments fueled by his regrets about selling out to a "rich bitch."[31] Ernest uses the people he has met and the experiences he has had during his marriage to Pauline to describe Harry's fears and regrets and seems to question whether he, too, is rotting away.

Like Ernest, Harry is a writer worried about the quality and quantity of his writing. As he contemplates death, he regrets not writing about his time in Paris, just as Ernest may have regretted never writing, at least at that point, his Paris book:

> He remembered the good times with them all, and the quarrels. They always picked the finest places to have the quarrels. And why had they always quarreled when he was feeling best? He had never written any of that because, at first, he never wanted to hurt any one and then it seemed as though there was enough to write without it. But he had always thought that he would write it finally. There was so much to write.[32]

Like Ernest, he worries about the changes he has seen during his lifetime and if his writing adequately describes what he has seen and experienced:

> He had seen the world change; not just the events; although he had seen many of them and had watched the people, he had seen the subtler change and he could remember how the people were at different times. He had been in it and he had watched it and it was his duty to write of it; but now he never would.[33]

Like Ernest, Harry is married to a wealthy woman and wonders if the comfortable life she provides is detrimental to his writing. Helen, Harry's wife, has generously put her wealth at his disposal to further his career. Yet Harry knows "the people he knew now were all much more comfortable when he did not work."[34] He blames Helen for his failure to write and for leaving "your own people, your goddamned old Westbury, Saratoga, Palm Beach people to take me on," saying, "your damned money was my armour."[35] Harry argues with Helen, attempting to blame her for drifting away from genuine people, and instead choosing to live comfortably among the rich. He complains that, "The rich were dull and they drank too much, or they played too much backgammon. They were dull and they were repetitious."[36] The story reflects Ernest's own personal and professional ambitions and fears and ends with Harry literally and symbolically rotting away with gangrene.

By the time Ernest was thirty-six, life's experiences in Key West, as well as Oak Park and Paris, had shown him the differences between the rich, the poor, and those in between. Ernest's early short stories reflected his personal adventures and his family's love of the outdoors. His experiences with Native Americans in Michigan helped him to embrace a sense of self-reliance and admire the simple beauty of the natural world. His boyhood experiences gave him the skills as well as the tenacity to explore life in the mountains above Lake Geneva (Lac Leman), pursue deep-sea fishing in the Gulf Stream, and survive in a tent while pursuing big game in Africa.

Living frugally with Hadley, he used the Paris years to cull content from his personal experiences and hone his craft as a writer. His belief in the value of hard work contributed to his early success. Combined with his self-confidence, he didn't give up but rather adhered to a strict work schedule and what would become a lifelong ritual for the process of writing.

Then he was seduced by money. After the success of *The Sun Also Rises* and *A Farewell to Arms*, Ernest increasingly associated with celebrities and people of wealth. In Paris, Ernest met F. Scott Fitzgerald, who thought "the very rich are different from you and me," traveled with Gerald and Sara Murphy, and fell in love with Pauline. In Key West, he quickly accepted the soft life provided by Pauline and her household staff; the house, car, and African safari provided by Uncle Gus; and the freedom to write without the worry of having to provide for his wife and children. His early interests in hunting and fishing evolved into adventures that required money and leisure time, and he began to spend more and more time in the company of the rich. Though he believed that wealth often corrupted writers and often spoke badly of the rich, he still enjoyed their company and their pastimes.

However, the poverty brought on by the Depression penetrated the bubble of comfortable isolation Ernest was enjoying in Key West. He became annoyed that his quiet fishing village was now filled with federal bureaucrats who were using Federal Emergency Relief Act funds to promote tourism and administer New Deal reforms that required people to do hard work for insufficient pay while robbing them of their dignity. He eventually reflected his growing awareness and discomfort with the unequal financial and social strata in *To Have and Have Not*.

Ernest tells the story of Harry Morgan, a Depression-era charter boat captain, who is forced by dire economic forces into the black-market activity of running contraband between Cuba and Florida. A wealthy fishing charter customer cheats Harry by slipping away without paying after a three-week fishing trip, leaving Harry destitute. Stuck in Havana and motivated by the need to support his family, Harry turns to crime and begins to ferry different types of illegal cargo between Cuba and Florida. In the novel, Ernest juxtaposes the depravity and hunger of the poor residents of Key West (the "have nots") against the soft, comfortable lives of wealthy yacht owners, the "haves."

Characters are based on people Ernest met in Key West—the working class he encountered on the docks and at Sloppy Joe's, the rich who moored their boats in Key West harbor, and the illegal Chinese immigrants who were being smuggled from Cuba to Key West to promote tourism in newly formed Chinatowns. The working men, such as Harry Morgan, are decent people who care about their families and are willing to work to support them, but are driven to desperate, violent, and criminal actions because of the Depression. Harry justifies his illegal actions because "I've got family . . . [and] I'm broke."[37]

While the "have nots" are presented with sympathy and understanding, the "haves" are portrayed as insensitive opportunists. Some have made their fortunes in businesses similar to Uncle Gus's Sloan's Liniment enterprise, "selling something everybody used by the millions of bottles, which cost three cents a quart to make."[38] Others, such as Harry Carpenter, live on trust funds and will survive even if they are "dropped from 5500 feet without a parachute," because they will "land safely with (their) knees under some rich man's table."[39] Married couples, such as Tommy and Helene Bradley, are modeled after Grant and Jane Mason. The thinly veiled Jane Mason is transformed into the sexually promiscuous Helene, who "collected writers as well as their books,"[40] and her husband, Tommy, a thinly disguised Grant Mason, who meekly obeys her orders to get out when he finds her in bed with a lover.

Ernest came to understand the "rich bitch" mentality, but he also saw that some women were simply used. He further captures the insensitivity of the "haves" in the story of the grain merchant, who used his wife's money to get started, had treated her well until the money he had made was double her original capital, and then "could afford to take no notice of her."[41]

Ernest's experiences with "the rich" and his disgust with Federal Emergency Relief Act and the Roosevelt administration propelled him into social commentary. In *To Have and Have Not*, he continued to write about the good, the bad, and the ugly, but rather than just focusing on the moral erosion of a lost generation, he writes about a town that has been transformed from a tropical paradise to a land of inequality and corruption, and a population in which the pleasure-seeking "haves" take advantage of the "have nots." As with his other novels, Ernest used his personal experiences and friendships to develop the plot and the characters. His marriage to Pauline and his travels with the Fitzgeralds and the Murphys gave him new insights into the thoughts and habits of the rich, and the financial support provided by Pauline and Uncle Gus gave him an understanding of the protection and security that accompanies life with a trust fund. However, while Ernest shares his thoughts about the unequal distribution of wealth, *To Have and Have Not* offers no solutions. The plot of the novel argues for social and political changes to help the working man, but the New Deal remedies were not a solution for Ernest. As a result, the fate of Harry Morgan outlines the limits of personal freedom, self-reliance, and hard work in Depression-era Key West. The

Figure 4.10. Ernest with Jack "Bumby" and Patrick "Mouse" Hemingway.
"Nothing's really happening to me here . . . I've got to get out."
Ernest Hemingway Collection. John F. Kennedy Presidential Library and Museum, Boston, Massachusetts.

closest Ernest comes to a solution is for Harry to say, "No matter how a man alone ain't got no f------ chance."[42]

Ernest's concern about the country's basic values and his personal conflict over money were real and troubling to him. His personal solution was to leave Key West, re-emerge himself in a life of action, and return to war. Harry in "The Snows of Kilimanjaro" was literally rotting away from gangrene, but Harry's rotting condition and words of regret also reflected Ernest's mid-life, mid-career fears. Was he truly afraid of nothing, or was he afraid that he, too, was rotting away under the protective shield of Pauline's wealth? Trips to Spain and safaris to Africa had been exciting diversions from the comfortable Key West life, but they had not produced the quality of thought and the preciseness of writing that were the result of the earlier relationships and experiences encountered Italy, France, and Spain. Now he now had a host of friends, wealthy, famous, and influential. They admired his daring adventures, his literary fame, and his good-natured storytelling. However, in a letter to Matthew Josephson, he admitted he had a nice boat and a beautiful house in Key West, but summarized his life by saying, "I could stay on here forever, but it's a soft life. Nothing's really happening to me here and I've got to get out."[43] His escape route was charted by a young, blonde writer named Martha Gellhorn. The destination was Spain.

Martha

Figure 5.1. Martha Gellhorn.
"young, pretty, college graduate, good home, more or less Junior League background, with a touch of exquisite Paris clothes and 'esprit' thrown in."[1]
Ernest Hemingway Collection. John F. Kennedy Presidential Library and Museum, Boston, Massachusetts.

LEAVING KEY WEST WAS THE REMEDY FOR THE ROUTINE ERNEST could not tolerate. He recognized that both his life and writing needed action. Family life had become too comfortable, and he knew the adventures of big-game hunting and deep-sea fishing were just calculated diversions. He showed his restlessness in *To Have and Have Not*. The "pleasant, dull and upright" family asleep on one of the yachts in the harbor were openly reflective of Pauline's family, and his interest in a new woman was voiced in his warning to women who expected their men to be monogamous.[2] He justified infidelity, saying:

> [Men] aren't built that way. They want some one new, or some one younger, or some one that they shouldn't have, or some one that looks like some one else. Or if you're dark they want a blonde. Or if you're blonde they go for a redhead. Or if you're a redhead then it's something else. . . . You can't blame them if that's the way they are.[3]

Knowing he had accepted and benefited from the generosity of Pauline and Uncle Gus, he also rationalized, "The better you treat a man and the more you show him you love him they quicker he gets tired of you."[4] Then he wrote and explained to Pauline's parents that, "you can't preserve your happiness by putting it away in moth balls" and that, "for a long time me and my conscience both have known I had to go to Spain," adding, "I'm very grateful to you both for providing Pauline who's made me happier than I've ever been."[5]

Ernest's call to action was also enhanced by the economic and political turmoil that surrounded him. The United States was engulfed in the Depression, and the democratic government of his beloved Spain was being threatened by a Fascist revolution. Yet life in Key West allowed his disengagement from these economic and social crises as well as the time and money to pursue bullfighting, big-game hunting, and deep-sea fishing. While he was pursuing his personal adventures or telling stories at the bar at Sloppy Joe's, his literary contemporaries were writing about significant political and social causes.

Ernest's personal solution was to re-emerge himself in a life of action and return to war. The success of *A Farewell to Arms* convinced him that love and war were good topics for a novel. Though his experiences in World War I had altered his views of war from those of his grandfathers', he wanted to explore how men could show honor and courage given the challenges of modern warfare. His passion was writing, and he believed war was the perfect venue to study men facing difficult situations. He wanted to be in a setting where he could observe men facing death and analyze their reactions to it.

Ernest's fascination with men in the face of death had fueled his fascination with bullfighting, and his many trips to Spain made him sensitive to Spain's political environment. Now there was disagreement on who should lead the country and what reforms, if any, should be enacted. Though there had been a democratic election, the results were being challenged and the count down to a civil war had begun. As Ernest had predicted, a civil war broke out in Spain in 1936 when a group of influential generals led by General Francisco Franco carried out a coup d'etat to oust the democratically elected Republican, Manuel Azaña. The conflict was viewed as struggle between social classes, between religious beliefs, between dictatorship and republican democracy, and between fascism and communism. The Republican/Loyalists believed it was a conflict between tyranny and freedom. The Nationalists believed it was a conflict between Christian civilization and Communism and lawlessness. History has shown it was the dress rehearsal for World War II.

Ernest felt the same call to action he experienced when he was eighteen and wanted to leave Kansas City and go to Italy. Only now he wanted to go to Spain; he needed to be part of the action. To his delight, and Pauline's dismay, he accepted an offer from the North American Newspaper Alliance (NANA) to cover the civil war in Spain as a war correspondent. By the time Ernest got to Spain, the Spanish Civil War had been underway for over a year, and he was itching to get involved. In September 1936, he had told his editor, Max Perkins: "I hate to have missed this Spanish thing worse than anything in the world but have to have this book (To Have and Have Not) finished first."[6] Finally, on March 16, 1937, he arrived in Spain as an accredited war correspondent for the NANA. For over a year, he covered the bloody conflict, often under fire, writing thirty-one dispatches for publication in European, Canadian, and American newspapers.

Ernest's interest in going to Spain was heightened by his encounter with Martha Gellhorn. In December 1936, Martha Gellhorn entered Sloppy Joe's, knowing that Ernest probably would be there. At twenty-eight, the attractive blonde already had traveled extensively in Spain, France, and Germany; had written articles for *The New Republic*, the *St. Louis Post-Dispatch*, and the Paris edition of *Vogue*; and had received national recognition for her accounts of despair and suffering during the Depression in her book, *The Trouble I've Seen*. She, too, was from St. Louis, where her father had been an obstetrician. Yet, despite the obvious similarities of being the child of an obstetrician as was Ernest, being from St. Louis and having attended Bryn Mawr as did Hadley, and having spent time in Paris working for *Vogue* as did Pauline, the real attraction was Ernest and Martha's mutual interest in the political climate of Spain.

When they met, Madrid was under siege and atrocities were being committed by both the Loyalists and the Nationalists. Ernest's eagerness to get back into the action and Martha's desire to report on the war firsthand created a bond between them. They talked all afternoon at Sloppy Joe's while Pauline awaited Ernest's arrival for a dinner with guests. Eventually, Pauline sent Charles Thompson to fetch Ernest, but Thompson returned, saying that Ernest had been delayed by "a beautiful blonde in a black dress."[7]

During the spring and fall of 1937, Ernest made four trips to Spain as a war correspondent for NANA and engaged in a life of risk with Martha. Ernest encouraged Martha to write, and when *Collier's* published her article, "Only the Shells Whine," she, too, became a bona fide war correspondent, thus initiating a rivalry between them as competing war correspondents and authors.

Martha didn't cater to Ernest as Hadley and Pauline had, but they developed a bond in the face of danger. They lived in the Hotel Florida, which was in the direct line of fire from heavy artillery, and traveled together to the frontlines in an armored car that was the target of machine gun fire. Martha learned to respect Ernest's knowledge of the battlefield and his ability to navigate booby traps, and he began to believe she was the bravest person he had ever met, including himself. It became obvious to the other journalists at the Hotel Florida that they were sleeping together when a shell hit the hotel in the middle of the night, and they fled their room together.

Madrid was under assault, and each day was filled with danger and death in the streets. Writers and journalists from around the world converged on the scene. Ernest supported the Loyalist cause because he believed it would bring a better life to the ordinary people of Spain and because the Nationalists were supported by the Fascists. Ernest's dislike of fascism went back to 1922 when he first reported on Mussolini's rise to power and called him "the biggest bluff in Europe."[8] Martha, too, supported the Loyalist cause and participated in Ernest's most dangerous assignments.

The Spanish Civil War pitted the Loyalists, who were supported by Russia, against Franco's Nationalists, who were supported by Germany and Italy. The Loyalists were loyal to the democratically elected Republican government. Stalin and Russian Communists provided soldiers and military equipment, but the Loyalists received less support from Russia than the Nationalist rebels, who benefited from the superior military equipment provided by Hitler and larger numbers of troops provided Mussolini.

The war inspired both sides not only to fight passionate battles and force political division, but also to commit many atrocities. Organized purges were carried out in territories captured by Franco's Nationalist forces because the rebel Nationalists feared national fragmentation and opposed separatist movements. They viewed the purging of leftists from Spain as a political necessity that was required to re-establish the monarchy and remove the Second Republic democracy. The Nationalists were motivated by the notion of social cleansing defined by their anti-communist views and their strong Catholic convictions. They supported the Spanish clergy, and one of their principal objectives was to confront the anti-clericalism of the Republican regime and defend the Catholic Church, which had been blamed by the Republicans for the country's ills. The Nationalists targeted Republican women with the overall goal of keeping them in their traditional place in Spanish society and promoted a campaign of humiliation and rape. Warnings were given over the radio that "immodest" women with Loyalist sympathies would be raped by Moorish troops. These rapes were not the result of soldiers disobeying orders, but rather official Nationalist policies.

Mass executions also took place in areas controlled by the Loyalists. At the outset of the war, seven thousand clergy were killed and churches were burned. Common to the political purges of both the Loyalists and the Nationalists were the sacas, whereby prisoners were taken from jails and prisons and taken for a paseo or ride to a mass execution. Most of the men and women taken from prisons and jails by the Loyalists were killed by death squads from the trade unions. One of the Loyalist justifications for the executions of the Nationalists was reprisal for their aerial bombings of civilians.

The drama and excitement of the war, his interest in Martha, and the companionship and stimulation from fellow writers mirrored the productive times Ernest spent in Europe fifteen years earlier. But now, Ernest was a writer with an extraordinary reputation and a visible, meaningful spokesman for the Loyalist cause. *Newsweek* published a story that his fee being one dollar per word was the highest ever paid a war correspondent, and his affiliation with NANA meant that his articles would circulate in some sixty newspapers, among them *The New York Times*, the *San Francisco Chronicle*, and the *Kansas City Star*. Herbert Matthews, a seasoned *New York Times* correspondent, praised Ernest's articles, saying that he represented "much that is brave and good and fine in a somewhat murky world."[9]

During the first few months of the war, both armies were joined by high numbers of Spanish volunteers, Nationalists by some one hundred thousand men and Loyalist Republicans by some 120,000. Many non-Spaniards, often affiliated with communist or socialist entities, also joined the International Brigades, believing that the Spanish Republic was a frontline in the war against fascism. The International Brigades represented the largest foreign contingent of those fighting for the Loyalist cause.

Figure 5.2. Ernest Hemingway in Madrid during the Spanish Civil War.
*Ernest Hemingway Collection. John F. Kennedy Presidential Library and
Museum, Boston, Massachusetts.*

Americans fought in the XV International Brigade. Many of the volunteers were communists or Soviet sympathizers. All were united by their hatred of fascism. Using the name of Abraham Lincoln, the Americans initially fielded three companies, two infantry and one machine gun. After less than two months of training, the Lincoln Brigade went into action in February 1937. Many of the Americans in the International Brigade were students and had never seen military service. Usually used as shock troops, they often led the attacks and suffered a high number of casualties. By the end of the war, the Lincoln Brigade had lost more than 20 percent of its strength.

Their commander, Robert Hale Merriman, became Ernest's model for Robert Jordan in *For Whom the Bell Tolls*. He was a doctoral student in economics at the University of California and was interested in Stalinism and the emerging economics in the Soviet Union. Earning a scholarship to study for one year in Moscow, he joined the anti-Fascist movement and left for Spain before his year was finished, convinced that defeating the Fascists in Spain and then Germany would prevent a second World War. Toward the end of the Spanish Civil War, Merriman led the Lincoln-Washington Battalion, which was badly beaten at the Battle of Belchite and forced to retreat toward Catalonia. As the troops passed through the town of Corbera d'Ebre, Merriman, as well as other American officers, were captured. A few hours later, he and the other officers were executed.

Both during and after the Spanish Civil War, the United States considered members of the Abraham Lincoln brigade supporters of the Soviet Union. In 1940, individuals in Detroit who had fostered the enlistment of Americans to serve in the Spanish Civil War were arrested on charges that they had violated the Neutrality Act. Though the charges were eventually dropped, Ernest challenged the Federal Bureau of Investigation (FBI) by signing a petition protesting the arrests. However, when the United States entered World War II, the FBI continued their attack on the veterans of the Lincoln Battalion by denying military promotion to prevent communists from rising in the armed forces. FBI Director J. Edgar Hoover specifically requested that President Roosevelt ensure that former Abraham Lincoln Brigade members fighting in US forces in

Figure 5.3. Martha Gellhorn with Robert Hale Merriman during the Spanish Civil War. Ernest Hemingway Collection. John F. Kennedy Presidential Library and Museum, Boston, Massachusetts.

World War II not be considered for commissions as officers or have any type of positive distinction conferred upon them. When World War II ended, Abraham Lincoln Brigade veterans were denied government jobs. Then in 1947, the Abraham Lincoln Brigade was placed on the Attorney General's List of Subversive Organizations, and the House Un-American Activities Committee blacklisted the Abraham Lincoln Brigade veterans and labeled them as communists.

Ernest initially went to Spain to report on the Spanish Civil War for the NANA, but as his time in Spain increased, so did his associations with Communist writers and sympathizers. Ernest met the Russian-trained staff officers headquartered at Gaylord's Hotel in Madrid and developed relationships with Russian Communists who could provide firsthand information for his articles. In addition to Merriman, he also became friends with US volunteers fighting on the Republican side and communist volunteers and journalists, including Ilya Ehrenburg, Gustav Regler, Gusavo Duran, and Mikhail Koltsov. Ernest was drawn to these men because of their mutual hatred of fascism and their common belief in the power of the pen.

Mikhail Koltsov, a close associate of Joseph Stalin, was sent from Russia in 1936 to cover the Spanish Civil War for *Pravda*, the official newspaper of the Communist Party in the Soviet Union, and with the help of Stalin became one of the most important journalists in the Soviet Union. When Ernest was invited to Gaylord's Hotel to have drinks with Koltzov, Martha accompanied him in what she called a "tag-along role."[10] She recalled in her *Memory* article that Ernest was excited about this rare invitation to Gaylord's and the opportunity to meet Koltzov, saying "No one in our little buddy circle of correspondents had been inside Gaylords or met Koltzov."[11] According to Martha, Ernest said, Koltzov was "officially the *Pravda* correspondent in Madrid but really he was Stalin's man, Stalin's eyes and ears on the spot."[12]

Also attending the gathering at Koltsov's suite at Gaylord's was General Juan Modesto. Young and aggressive, he was considered the most talented general in the Republican army. As the evening progressed, Ernest became irritated at Martha's conversing with Modesto and the attention she was receiving from the younger, "intensely attractive" general, and he

Figure 5.4. Ernest Hemingway with Ilya Ehrenburg and Gustav Regler during the Spanish Civil War.

Ilya Ehrenburg was a Soviet writer, Bolshevik revolutionary, journalist, and historian and one of the most prolific and notable authors in the Soviet Union. As an outspoken anti-Fascist reporter during the First World War and Spanish Civil War, his articles were known to provoke controversy and were banned in Germany.

Gustav Regler was a German Socialist novelist who served in the German infantry during the First World War and then joined the Communist Party, spent time in the Soviet Union, and later served as political commissar of the XII International Brigade during the Spanish Civil War. While in Spain, he wrote articles as a special correspondent for the *Deutsche Zentral Zeitung*, the German-language newspaper published in Moscow by the German-speaking section of the Communist International.

Ernest Hemingway Collection. John F. Kennedy Presidential Library and Museum, Boston, Massachusetts.

challenged Modesto to a duel. As the two men headed for the door and prepared to play Russian roulette each with a revolver containing one bullet, Koltzov observed the conflict and separated the men. Ernest and Martha were ushered to the door and not invited back.

Later in the war, Ernest and Martha saw Modesto again at his command post on the front. Though it was unheard of for journalists to visit a general at his command post, Ernest and Martha made their way to the front, eager to report on the action. According to Martha, Ernest asked Modesto technical, tactical questions, as of one general to another. Modesto's brief answers were tactically traditional and based on Stalinist orthodoxy, and the conversation was punctuated by the loud explosions of a mortar attack. As the explosions grew louder and closer, it became clear to Martha that Ernest and Modesto were playing Russian roulette with mortar bombs. Neither man would lose face by moving first. It took the urging of a military advisor attached to Modesto's staff to tell the group to move out of harm's way.

Ernest and Martha's interest in meeting the Russian journalists and maneuvering their way to the frontlines was based on their mutual desire to get firsthand details for their articles. Ernest, however, had another quest. He wanted to test his own courage in the face of danger. He told British poet Steven Spender, who joined the writers and journalists in Spain in 1937, that his principal reason for coming to Spain was to discover "whether he had lost his nerve under the conditions of warfare."[13] He relished the role of the old war veteran and specifically sought situations to test his courage. He repeatedly exposed himself to enemy fire and often called attention to the risks he was taking to get his stories, saying "this correspondent has been doing the most dangerous thing you can do in this war. That is, keep close behind an unstabilized line where the enemy is attacking with mechanized forces."[14]

Impressed with his devotion to the Loyalist cause, his experience and understanding of the tactical aspects of war, and his easy fluency in Spanish, Martha was at Ernest's side in all his risk-taking adventures. He was her guide and teacher. She was happy being his lover but not interested in being his wife, believing that the demands he would make as her husband would be different from the ones he would make as her lover.

Martha liked the companionship they shared and his political allegiance to Spain, and she respected his literary genius. She later said, "I think it was the only time in his life, when he was not the most important thing there was. He really cared about the Republic, and he cared about that war. I believe I never would've gotten hooked otherwise."[15]

Ernest's articles revealed his disgust with the Fascists for preying on innocent victims. His April 11, 1937, NANA dispatch, "The Shelling of Madrid," detailed not only the "legitimate" shelling of military targets, but also the shelling of innocent Sunday promenaders. "They killed an old woman returning from market dropping her in a huddled black heap of clothing, with one leg, suddenly detached, whirling against the wall of an adjoining house."[16] In the same article he describes a car being hit, and "the driver lurch[ing] out, his scalp hanging down over his eyes, to sit down on the side with his hand against his face, the blood making a smooth sheen down over his chin."[17] He also showed great sympathy for the refugees who were driven from their homes by the war. In "The Flight of the Refugees," he tells of a woman riding a mule holding a red-faced baby that could not have been two days old. "The mother's head swung steadily up and down with the motion of the beast she rode, and the baby's jet-black hair was drifted gray with the dust. A man led the mule forward . . . 'When was the baby born?' I asked him as our car swung alongside. 'Yesterday,' he said proudly."[18]

The war was one of the hardest Spain ever faced and left the country in shambles. Over a million men died, and the number of wounded was immense. Factories were destroyed, railways needed renovation, forests were cut down, herds of cattle were slaughtered, and the orange and olive groves became barren. In addition to the extreme loss of life during the war, there were daily executions after the war. Anyone suspected of volunteering to serve the Republic in any capacity, whether civil or military, was classified as a "Red" and, if not executed, sentenced to fifteen to thirty years of penal servitude in a forced labor camp. The destruction caused by Nationalist artillery and by German and Italian bombers in Madrid, Barcelona, and elsewhere was attributed to the "Reds."

Both Ernest and Martha had vigorously supported the losing Republican side and were politically out of favor in Spain. However, both continued to express their sympathy for the plight of the common people in their writing. Though Ernest eventually would gain wealth and notoriety with *For Whom the Bell Tolls*, his journalism reflected his deep concern for the plight of the Spanish people. He had recorded the plight of refugees in his NANA dispatches and now articulated his concerns in articles found in publications with Communist ties.

Ernest continued to support the Loyalist effort by accepting a 1938 commission from the Soviet newspaper *Pravda* and wrote a vitriolic attack on fascism. "The Barbarism of Fascist Interventionists in Spain" describes the "murder done in Spain by the Fascist invaders."[19] Ernest reacts with anger to the Fascists' "deliberate bombing of innocent people" and the timing of "their bombardments for the hours when the people leave the cinema to go to their homes."[20] As in the articles he wrote for NANA, he describes in gruesome detail the attacks on the civilian population. He writes about the shelling of a streetcar in Madrid filled with workers and comments on their suffering from hunger. Describing a dog sniffing about in the wreckage and running off with a large piece of human intestine trailing from its jaws, he says, "He was hungry, as everyone else is in Madrid."[21]

As the Loyalist front crumbled, Martha visited hospitals and wrote reports about food lines that stretched for blocks and near famine conditions in the hospitals. She described Barcelona, as "a whole city starving to death" with hospital wards "filled with beautiful small children wounded in the daily air-raids" as well as "children wounded by hunger."[22] Food was scarce during the war, and by the end, it was almost nonexistent. These children were fed "soup that was only hot water with a few green leaves and a few slivers of grey meat floating in it, and a small piece of bread, war bread, made of sawdust or sand."[23]

Before she left Europe, *Collier's* sent Martha to Czechoslovakia. Having experienced the power of Germany in Spain, she knowingly recorded the naiveté of the Czech people. She wrote about the optimism of the rural population, saying, "As the Czech Army mobilized . . . with their splendid equipment roll[ing] along the roads to take up position in their fortifications on the border, the people lined the roads and cheered them and threw flowers, and the soldiers sang and waved."[24] She went on to say that:

> In Prague the mood was sober and determined. The nation was united, ready to defend their admirable state, no matter what it cost. (There was a) marvelous feeling of will; no panic about Hitler. They counted on themselves, their armaments factories, their iron and coal, their wheat. They were practical, steady people and they did not believe that Hitler was some kind of invincible superman.[25]

But later, when England and France appeased Hitler by withdrawing their commitment to Czechoslovakia, forcing the Czech government to cede all the Sudetenland to Germany, she mourned the loss of democracy. She noted, "Now the awful silence was beginning here, the silence that was the sound of doom, and fear where there had been none."[26] Martha left Czechoslovakia on the last civilian plane, carrying secret documents that testified to the Nazi terror. Like Ernest, her experiences in Spain and later Czechoslovakia fortified her resolve to fight fascism. She believed:

> I have a wonderful and privileged life and am deeply aware every minute of my benefits and good luck. But that doesn't let me out. Or maybe that is what lets me in . . . the only way I can pay back for what fate and society have handed me is to try, in minor totally useless ways, to make an angry sound against injustice.[27]

When it became apparent that the Fascists would win in Spain, NANA released Ernest from his assignment, but Martha continued to write for *Collier's*. When they returned to Havana in 1939, both were convinced the Spanish Civil War was merely a prelude to a larger global conflict. Ernest, Martha, their fellow writers, and the many Loyalist soldiers sensed they were fighting more than just Fascism in Spain. In April 1938, Martha had told Eleanor Roosevelt, "What goes on here (Spain) seems to me very much the affair of all of us, who do not want a world whose Bible is Mein Kampf."[28] In a July 1938 article for *Ken*, Ernest had publicly asked President Roosevelt to provide aid to Spain, but Roosevelt continued his policy of nonintervention.

Later in an August article for *Pravda*, Ernest said the German "bombs are very good. They have learned much in their experimenting in Spain and their bombing is getting better every time," and predicted that "The crimes committed by Fascism will raise the world against it."[29] Ernest believed that war would break out within a year. On September 1, 1939, Hitler unleashed the blitzkrieg against Poland.

As planned, Ernest used the friendships and personal experiences he had collected during the Spanish Civil War in a new novel, and he and Martha went to Sun Valley, Idaho, where much of the novel was written. Though Ernest and Martha were united in their commitment to the Loyalist cause and the novel was dedicated to Martha Gellhorn, her only presence in the book is found in the physical description of the character, Maria:

> She had high cheek bones, merry eyes and a straight mouth with full lips. Her hair was the golden brown of a grain field. . . . Her legs slanted long and clean from the open cuffs of the trousers . . . every time Robert Jordan looked at her he could feel a thickness in his throat. . . . She moved awkwardly as a colt moves, but with that same grace as of a young animal.[30]

However, the friendships and experiences from their time in Spain were used to create a realistic setting, an engaging plot, and memorable characters. The Andalusian town of Ronda, where a political massacre that killed over five hundred Nationalists occurred during the first month of the war, is used for the novel's setting and the three days of conflict that drive the plot. The main character, Robert Jordan, is modeled after Robert Merriman, the American doctoral student who left his research in the Soviet Union to become a commander in the Abraham Lincoln Brigade and was captured and killed after the final assault on Belchite. In describing Jordan's commitment to the Loyalist cause, Ernest mirrors his, as well as Martha's, commitment to fighting Fascism with almost religious intensity, saying:

It was a feeling of consecration to a duty toward all the oppressed of the world which would be as difficult and embarrassing to speak about as religious experience and yet it was authentic as the feeling you had when you heard Bach or stood in Chartres Cathedral or the Cathedral at Leon and saw the light coming through the great windows. . . . It gave you a part in something that you could believe in wholly and completely. . . . It was something that you had never known before but that you had experienced now and you gave such importance to it and the reasons for it that your own death seemed of complete unimportance. . . . But the best thing was that there was something you could do about this feeling. . . . You could fight.[31]

In the novel, as in the war, the Fascists prevail. At the climax of the novel, Robert Jordan prepares for his own death as the Fascist cavalry approaches. He is injured but has a sub-machine gun and waits to engage the enemy so that they have no choice but to shoot him. Given the choice between death or capture and torture, Jordan courageously faces death and is a model of grace under pressure. He knows, "I have fought for what I believed in for a year now. If we win here we will win everywhere. The world is a fine place and worth the fighting for and I hate very much to leave it."[32] Like Pedro Romaro in *The Sun Also Rises* and Fredric Henry in *A Farewell to Arms*, Robert Jordan lives in a violent, dangerous world. As a code hero, he behaves honorably while suffering injuries and confronting death, thus proving his value as courageous man in a brutal world. He is free-willed, individualistic, adventuresome, and looks at death squarely in the eyes.

While Grandfather Anson Hemingway instilled Ernest with a sense of honor and courage that he had found in battle, the rules of battle changed by the time Ernest was old enough to participate. The romantic conceptions of the ancient art of war—hand-to-hand combat, sportsmanlike competition—that Ernest had learned from his grandfather were no longer valid in the post–World War I world. As a passive victim of an exploding Austrian mortar shell in the Italian trenches, Ernest learned that the rules had changed. After his experiences in Italy, he endeavored to show how a victim of modern weaponry could also be a courageous hero. Like Robert Jordan, they "learned the dry-mouthed, fear-purged, surging ecstasy of battle and . . . fought . . . for all the poor in the world, against all the tyranny, for all the things that you believed and for the new world that you had been educated into."[33]

Ernest enabled his readers to understand and feel the fear and danger his characters faced by using imagery associated with modern armament to produce an atmosphere of violence and death. Major images in *For Whom the Bell Tolls* are the sights of the automatic weaponry and the sounds of the superior aircraft associated with the Nationalists. The Fascist planes are especially dreaded. With the sound of their approach, there is a sense of foreboding felt by the characters in the novel as well as the reader. Hope vanishes, and commitment and abilities become meaningless. No longer does the best soldier win, but rather the soldier with the biggest gun or the side with the most advanced and largest number of aircraft. Thus, a Hemingway hero, such as Robert Jordan, faces the ultimate reality, death, but exhibits grace under pressure, knowing he has fought for what he believes with honor and courage.

Ernest understood that Spain's change from democracy to fascist dictatorship would affect everyone, not just Spaniards. He chose a title for his new novel from John Donne's series of meditations and prayers on health, pain, and sickness published in 1624 as *Devotions upon Emergent Occasions*, specifically "Meditation XVII." The title, *For Whom the Bell Tolls*, reinforces the themes of death and the importance of resisting the progression of Fascism, both of which weigh heavily in the war and in novel. Through the title Ernest reminds his readers that, "No man is an Island, intire of it selfe; every man is a piece of the Continent, a part of the maine," and that when the death bell tolls, as was the practice in the seventeenth century, "never send to know for whom the bell tolls; It tolls for thee."[34]

When Ernest left Key West and headed to Spain, he was looking for action and adventure and a set of experiences that would provide the material for a new novel that would seal his reputation as a gifted American writer. In leaving his comfortable life, his friends, and his family, he purposely sought out the dangers of war, controversial friendships, and an extramarital love affair with a woman who would become the next Mrs. Hemingway. In many ways, he got exactly what he was looking

Figure 5.5. Ernest Hemingway and Martha Gellhorn celebrating the publication of *For Whom the Bell Tolls* in New York.
Ernest Hemingway Collection. John F. Kennedy Presidential Library and Museum, Boston, Massachusetts.

for. *For Whom the Bell Tolls* was published in October 1940. Though the book was banned in Spain until 1958 and the Hollywood film based on the novel was not permitted to be shown in Spanish cinemas, by April 1941 almost five hundred thousand copies of the book were sold; Ernest was named as a finalist for the Pulitzer Prize; and in January 1942, the movie rights were purchased by Paramount for one hundred thousand dollars. Leaving home and pursuing a new adventure proved once again to be a success for Ernest. However, because of his commitment to the Soviet-supported Loyalist cause and his friendships with Communist writers, he earned the stigma of being a Communist. Though he would repeat numerous times for the rest of his life that he was not a Communist, but just hated Fascism, the label would remain.

Figure 5.6. Martha Gellhorn in Sun Valley, Idaho.
"Anyone confusing a handsome and ambitious girl with the Queen of Heaven should be punished as a fool."
Ernest Hemingway Collection. John F. Kennedy Presidential Library and Museum, Boston, Massachusetts.

When they left Spain in February 1939, Ernest and Martha returned to Key West and Havana. Though Ernest was still married to Pauline, he lived with Martha at the Hotel Biltmore Sevilla in Havana and maintained a façade of separation from Martha by posting and receiving mail at the Ambos Mundos Hotel in Havana. From Havana he commuted to Key West until November 1940, when Pauline divorced him on grounds of desertion. Ernest had been content to live at the Hotel Florida in Madrid, and before the divorce from Pauline was comfortable at the Biltmore Sevilla in Havana. He enjoyed the atmosphere of Old Havana and

Figure 5.7. Ernest Hemingway, Martha Gellhorn, and Mme Chiang Kai-shek in Chungking, China during the Sino-Japanese War.

Ernest Hemingway Collection. John F. Kennedy Presidential Library and Museum, Boston, Massachusetts.

the camaraderie he found in his favorite local bars, the Floridita and the Bogedita del Medio. His routine was intact. He'd write in the peace of his room in the morning and retreat to the bars or his boat in the afternoon.

Martha, however, found the hotel quarters cramped and decided to pursue a means to keep Ernest out of the local bars. Finca Vigia, Look-out Farm, met both of her objectives. The house needed work, but it had a swimming pool and a tennis court, and it was located a reasonable distance from Havana on fifteen acres of land. Martha began renovation of the house, finished her collection of short stories for Scribner's, and then concluded an agreement with *Collier's* to go to the Orient to report on the defenses of Hong Kong, Singapore, and the Dutch East Indies and look at the Burma Road to study the progress of the Sino-Japanese War. Though Ernest was reluctant to go to the Orient, Martha "was determined to see the Orient before (she) died or the world ended or whatever came next."[35]

Ernest had no experience with a woman who wanted to lead a life that was independent of his, but he took an assignment to write articles for *PM*, a new left-liberal New York newspaper, so that he could travel to the Orient with Martha. Then two weeks after his divorce from Pauline, he convinced Martha to marry him in Cheyenne, Wyoming, on November 21, 1940. Though Ernest openly stated, "What I wanted was a wife in bed at night not somewhere having even higher adventures at so many thousand bucks the adventure," Martha's focus was more on her career as a journalist than on being Mrs. Hemingway.[36]

After they were married, they spent their "working honeymoon" in the Orient. In Hong Kong, they met the widow of Sun Yat-sen, and then went to the front at Canton and later to Chungking, the wartime capital. In Chungking, they met with Generalissimo and Madame Chiang Kai-shek as well as the American ambassador to discuss China's military and political situation.

Martha's articles for *Collier's* focused on the political and military aims of China and the adequacy of military defenses in Hong Kong, Singapore, the Dutch East Indies, and the Burma Road. They also revealed her shock at the squalid, overcrowded conditions she and Ernest encountered in China. Recognizing Japan's threat, Ernest's articles for *PM*

Figure 5.8. Mr. and Mrs. Hemingway in Hawaii, 1941.

Hulton Archive/Getty Images

pointed out China's need for assistance in its struggle to repel aggression from Japan.

For both, the situation in China seemed reminiscent of Spain. There were numerous political agendas, fighting on many fronts, and the death of innocent Chinese from wartime executions, malnutrition, and starvation. Chiang Kai-shek had ended China's Warlord Era and worked toward unifying the country, but now was faced with fighting Communist infiltration of China as well as aggression from Japan. Chiang Kai-shek was relentless and brutal. In 1927, he purged China of thousands of suspected Communists via large-scale massacres, believing it better to kill one thousand innocent people rather than allowing one Communist to escape. Then in 1938 he supported the man-made Yellow River flood, which killed hundreds of thousands of innocent Chinese to fend off an advance from the Japanese, and supported China's Scorched Earth Policy by setting fires that left thousands of Chinese homeless or dead.

When Ernest and Martha returned to the United States from China, they were debriefed by Colonel John W. Thomason at the Office of Naval Intelligence in Washington, DC. In that meeting, Martha spoke of the inadequacies of the British defense system in Singapore while Ernest emphasized the strategic importance of providing support to Chiang Kai-shek. Ernest thought that a long ground war in China would engage a majority of the Japanese army and delay their drive into Southeast Asia, giving the United States time to build up a two-ocean navy that would be crucial to US national defense. Having stopped in Hawaii on their way to and from China, Ernest also mentioned that he was appalled by the lack of US preparation at Pearl Harbor.

In Hawaii, the divide between the two competing writers began to widen. Having been introduced to the island's customs of lei-draping and continuous entertaining, Ernest enjoyed the attention he received as a bestselling author and a literary icon, while Martha sought and wished for seclusion. She told her mother, "This is a place where hospitality is a curse, and no one can be alone."[37]

After the trip to the Orient and the meeting in Washington, DC, Ernest and Martha returned to Cuba, where they relaxed and enjoyed a new social life with members of the American Embassy in Cuba. The first secretary at the American Embassy, Robert Joyce and his wife, as well as the ranking officer Ellis Briggs and his wife, became friends and often went to the Finca for casual dinners and swimming parties. Eventually, however, Martha felt the need to get back to work and began a series of events where much of their married life was spent apart. Though Martha started the restoration of Finca Vigia, was a good stepmother to Ernest's three sons, and played the role of Mrs. Hemingway while in Cuba, she was an avid journalist and preferred life on the road.

As World War II escalated, Martha pursued assignments in the Caribbean and Europe for *Collier's*, but Ernest's correspondence reveals he didn't like being left alone. When Martha left the Finca to cover submarine warfare in the Caribbean, he wrote to Max Perkins, sarcastically saying, "She is at present navigating the Caribbean in a thirty-foot sloop with a 4' x 5' cabin with a 4' 5" head room, accompanied by three faithful negro followers. I understand that if she is lost at sea, *Collier's* will pay double for her last article. I expect they will also want me to write a Tribute to their intrepid correspondent."[38]

Then at the height of the war, in February 1944, Martha ventured to the Italian battlefront in Cassino to report on the fighting between Allied troops and German resistance. Cassino was a key point in the German winter defensive line, blocking the Allied advance to Rome. After Allied aircraft dropped fourteen hundred tons of bombs on Cassino, leaving the town so heaped with rubble that tanks could not operate until bulldozers cleared paths for them, the Allies did break through German lines and were able to take Rome. However, though Cassino was a dangerous and challenging assignment for Martha, Ernest shared neither the gravity nor the excitement of her assignment. He complained that she should be at home with him and sent her an angry telegram, saying, "ARE YOU A WAR CORRESPONDENT OR WIFE IN MY BED?"[39]

As the war progressed, Martha relished reporting on military conflicts, but her letters to Ernest show she was uncomfortable with their marital conflict. She longed for the days before they were married and said:

I wish we could stop it all now, the prestige, the possessions, the position, the knowledge. . . . I would like to be young and poor and in Madrid and with you and not married to you. . . . I think that I always wanted to feel in some way like a woman and if I ever did, it was the first winter in Madrid. There is a sort of blindness and fervor and recklessness about that sort of feeling which one must always want. I hate being so wise and so careful, so reliable, so denatured, so able to get on.[40]

Martha sensed that almost anything she said, even her letter, would anger Ernest: "I will almost bet twenty dollars that this letter makes you angry, doesn't it?' 'What does she mean?' you will say, 'complaining and crying for some other time and place and life?' 'What the hell is the matter with that bitch?'"[41]

Angry or not, being alone in Cuba compelled Ernest to explore a new series of friendships and adventures. His circle of friends broadened to include more officials at the American Embassy, and through them he developed a relationship with Spruille Braden, the American ambassador to Cuba. Like Ernest, Braden had become concerned about the loyalties of Spaniards living in Cuba. Both Ernest and the ambassador wondered, if Franco's Spain joined the Axis powers, which side of the war would the Cuban Spaniards support? Given Cuba's proximity to the United States and its history of revolution, Braden and Ernest conceived a plan to form a private intelligence network to conduct espionage on Falangist supporters of the Spanish fascist party and other Nazi sympathizers in Cuba.

With the full support of Braden, Ernest recruited a group of anti-Fascist agents and used the Finca's guest house as their secret headquarters. Information on the actions and any sabotage attempts of the pro-Nazi Falange, which threatened US interests was gathered by the agents and funneled to Ernest, who translated and processed it and then hand-delivered it to Robert Joyce at the Embassy. The code name for the group was Crime Shop, but Ernest called it the Crook Factory. Ernest eagerly accepted this new assignment and wrote to his editor, Max Perkins, who would have liked Ernest to write another bestselling novel, that he wanted to do something for the war effort. Organizing a spy ring was well suited to his personality and his need for adventure.

Given his new Crook Factory enterprise, Ernest recruited several of his friends from the Spanish Civil War, including a Catholic priest, known as Black Priest, who had served as a machine gunner on the Republican/Loyalist side, and the Russian Communist Loyalist Gustavo Duran. He also recruited professional jai-alai players and local waiters, bartenders, and fishermen. There were twenty-six informants in his spy ring: six working full-time and twenty working as part-time undercover agents. They were enlisted to keep an eye on the thousands of pro-Franco Spaniards in Cuba who were thought to have sided with the German-Italian Axis.

Though Ernest had the full support of the American ambassador, the Crook Factory activity initiated the beginning of his FBI file. The first entry in the file is a memorandum dated October 8, 1942, from R. Gordon Leddy, the legal attaché to the FBI stationed in Havana. In his memorandum to FBI Director J. Edgar Hoover, Leddy notes that Ernest has become friendly with Robert Joyce, the second secretary of the Embassy, and through him met American Ambassador Braden. Leddy explains that as a result of his friendship with Joyce and now Braden, the ambassador believes Ernest would be useful to the Embassy's intelligence program because of his "experience in the Spanish Civil War, his intimate acquaintances with Spanish Republican refuges in Cuba, as well as his long experience on the island."[42] Though the purpose of Leddy's memorandum was to acquaint Hoover with the relationship that was developing between Ernest and the ambassador, Leddy reveals his negative bias toward Ernest and his intelligence activities by mentioning that Ernest signed a declaration in 1940 that severely criticized the FBI for the arrests of individuals in Detroit, Michigan. The arrests were based on charges that the men had violated the Neutrality Act because they fostered the enlistment of Americans during the Spanish Civil War.

In an entry a day later, Leddy shares information with C. H. Carson in the Washington, DC, office that Martha Gellhorn, now Mrs. Hemingway, would be the personal guest of Mrs. Roosevelt in Washington, DC, and that the ambassador outlined to her "certain aspects of the intelligence situation in Cuba in order that she might convey the same in personal conversation, to the President and Mrs. Roosevelt."[43] The letter ends with the suggestion that Carson bring this information to the personal attention of Director J. Edgar Hoover.

Martha's friendship with Eleanor Roosevelt dated back to 1934 when she worked for Harry Hopkins as a relief-investigator for the Depression-era Federal Emergency Relief Administration and was sent to the depressed mill towns of New England and the South to examine how the unemployed were treated and managed to live. When she brought her first reports of the poverty, slow starvation, and utter despair of the families she interviewed to Hopkins, he introduced her to Mrs. Roosevelt, who in turn introduced her to the president. The Roosevelts were interested in and fascinated by Martha's riveting grassroots information and soon became her lifelong friends.

Martha's initial White House dinner invitation turned into an open invitation to return to the White House anytime to tell them more. Then, when Martha was fired for inciting a riot among unemployed workers in rural Idaho in 1934, Mrs. Roosevelt invited her to live at the White House until she found new employment. For two months, Martha stayed in the Lincoln bedroom and helped Mrs. Roosevelt answer the sheaves of mail she was receiving from people in dire straits. Eventually, this friendship would generate the June 1937 invitation for the White House showing of the Loyalist propaganda film *Spanish Earth* and prompted Mrs. Roosevelt to write in her daily column, "My Day," that, "Martha Gellhorn seems to have come back (from Spain) with one deep conviction . . . that the Spanish people are a glorious people and something is happening in Spain which may mean much to rest of the world."[44] Later in 1943, Ernest and Martha were invited to the White House to join President and Mrs. Roosevelt and a group of generals for a private viewing of the film *For Whom the Bell Tolls.*

Though Martha's friendship with the Roosevelts provided Ernest and Martha with easy access to the White House and government officials, the friendship was not a source of comfort for the FBI, especially J. Edgar Hoover, who had enormous power and a notorious need for control. Also, Ernest wasn't happy that Martha continued to leave him

Figure 5.9. Ernest Hemingway's *Pilar*, a thirty-eight-foot fishing boat disguised as a research vessel during World War II and used to search for German submarines.

Ernest Hemingway Collection. John F. Kennedy Presidential Library and Museum, Boston, Massachusetts.

alone to pursue her own career. He confessed to his son Patrick that he was "Going to get me somebody who wants to stick around with me and let me be the writer of the family."[45] Ernest was miserable as soon as he was left alone, and when *Collier's* sent Martha an assignment to cover the European Theater of Operations during World War II, he looked for new territory and another new adventure.

When German submarines were discovered in the Gulf of Mexico, Ernest requested and was granted permission to use the *Pilar* for coastal patrol and investigative work along the coast of Cuba. He transformed the *Pilar* into a spy ship camouflaged as a marine research vessel. The *Pilar* carried bazookas, explosives, machine guns, and radio equipment. Ernest hoped the *Pilar* would be halted by a German sub so his crew could attack the German crew with machine gun fire and destroy the sub with blasts from bazookas and by throwing hand grenades down the conning tower. FBI files indicate Ernest also received permission from Naval Attaché Colonel Hayne D. Boden, US Marine Corps, to check coastal waters off northern Cuba for the possibility of enemy submarine or clandestine radio activity and that he was accompanied on his boat by an employee of the Naval Attaché's office.[46]

While Ernest and his crew continued to go out for patrols during October and early November 1943, the *Pilar's* patrols for German submarines eventually came to an end. By October, convoys of Allied ships passed through Cuban waters without a single loss, and not a single German submarine was raised. The *Pilar's* patrols turned into fishing trips, and the grenades were thrown into the water in drunken sport. Ernest looked elsewhere for action and requested permission to operate the *Pilar* in Caribbean waters, using Guantanamo as a supply base. However, he never received clearance from the US Navy nor the embassy to begin patrols.

Though Ambassador Braden supported the patrols and said Ernest did an "A-one job" and Ernest and Martha enjoyed a friendship with Robert P. Joyce, second secretary of the American Embassy in Havana, Ernest's investigative efforts didn't have the support of his wife or the FBI. Martha saw the patrols as a mere ploy to get more rationed gasoline for the boat, and she was embarrassed by his exaggerated stories of his exploits and the obsequiousness of his admirers. She wanted him to go back to Europe where he could do some good in the war against Hitler. She badgered him about his idle life while she continued to pursue assignments for *Collier's*. Their time together became increasingly antagonistic, and young Gregory overheard Ernest tell Martha, "I'll show you, you conceited bitch. They'll be reading my stuff long after the worms have finished with you."[47]

Hoover's attitude toward Ernest's investigative efforts also remained negative. Hoover and his agents continued to resent Ernest's attack on the FBI early in 1940 and the general smear campaign following the arrests of individuals in Detroit charged with violation of federal statutes in connection with their participation in the Spanish Civil War. Numerous entries in Ernest's FBI file remind the reader that Ernest had signed the declaration severely criticizing the FBI and that he had been accused of being of Communist sympathy.

The patrols had met Ernest's need for adventure, stimulated his interest in military action, and nourished his love of the water. Yet, by the time his war game ended, he knew the Allied invasion of France was going to happen and he reluctantly decided to go back to journalism. Martha continued to beg him to come to Europe to share in the adventures of World War II. On December 12, 1943, she appealed to him as a writer, a novelist-historian, and as her husband. She said:

> You will feel deprived as a writer if this is all over and have not had a share in this . . . the place is crying out for you, not for immediate stuff but for the record. . . . I beg you to think this over very seriously. . . . I say this not only because I miss you and want you here, but I hate not sharing it with you. . . . It would be a terrible mistake to miss this, for both of us. . . . I would never be able to tell you about it because I could never do the things that you can. You would be the one who would see for us.[48]

Reluctantly, Ernest returned the *Pilar* to the harbor in Cojimar. He left Cuba to join Martha in Europe, but not without telling her that "had she allowed him to remain on patrol, a fine novel would have come out of his experiences, but now he would lose the story, for journalism would erase it from his head."[49] Then with his choice of any newspaper or magazine in the world, Ernest deliberately offered his services to *Collier's*. In March 1944, he wrote to *Collier's* editor Charles Colepaugh and enclosed a commendation from Ambassador Braden, which thanked Ernest for carrying out "highly confidential intelligence activities . . . involving personal risks and ever-present danger."[50] Then, because the US military did not want any female correspondents in Europe, and specifically forbade them from covering the Normandy invasion, *Collier's* made Ernest the leading correspondent in place of Martha. Though the US War Department ruling allowed women to go to war zones, they did not have accreditation to military units as required for admission to press camps at the front. Ambitious and hard-working, Martha was furious, and the end of their marriage was in sight. Martha knew she "was totally blocked . . . having taken *Collier's*, he automatically destroyed my chance of covering the fighting in an official capacity."[51] She told him "that he was making it impossible for (her) to go on loving him."[52]

With accreditation as a war correspondent, Ernest was able to report on D-Day. He went to a secret staging area and then boarded the attack transport *Dorothea L. Dix* on June 5. On the morning of June 6, he was transferred to a landing craft, and from his station beside the commander of the vessel witnessed the troops wade ashore at Omaha Beach. In his July 22, 1944, "Voyage to Victory" article for *Collier's*, he described for his readers the steep cliffs of Omaha Beach, the vantage points of the German machine guns along the lower ridges of the cliffs, and the drowning of hundreds of men as they tried to reach the shore under heavy machine gun fire. He admitted that, "Real war is never like paper war nor do accounts of it read much the way it looks. But if you want to know how it was in an LCV(P) on D-Day when we took Fox Green Beach and Easy Red Beach on the sixth of June 1944, then this is as near as I can come to it."[53]

Martha, however, managed to get aboard an unarmed hospital ship, lock herself in a toilet, and on the night of June 6, went ashore with the stretcher bearers to collect wounded men. Martha actually walked on the Normandy beachhead and picked her way through mine fields and barbed wire, while Ernest was confined to the bridge of a landing craft. Though she had no official papers and no travel orders, she faced the same dangers and hardships as soldiers. Harold Acton, the British literary historian, praised her articles as the best written and most acute of all the ones submitted to him. He concluded, "they compared favorably with the work of Ernest and that she was a good influence on him."[54]

After D-Day, both Ernest and Martha were in Paris, and Ernest insisted they have dinner together. Martha wanted to talk about a divorce, but Ernest had brought soldiers from his regiment and spent most of the evening insulting her. Though her coverage of the historic invasion was more detailed and informative than Ernest's, he discredited her story and was irritated that she had arrived on the Normandy beachhead before he did. Later, however, he sent her a note of apology and then met with her in London. According to Martha:

> Though he had previously refused even to talk of divorce, he then came to Yes, he would get the divorce in Cuba as I wanted. We were both residents, so it was easy and legal. I had no intention of leaving the war for weeks in Reno and I never dreamed of asking for anything—money, alimony. I was intensely eager for the divorce so that I could get my passport changed back to Gellhorn. I wanted to be free of him and his name; and step out of the whole picture fast.[55]

Their divorce was final on December 21, 1945, and they never saw each other again.

Mary

Figure 6.1. Mary Welsh Hemingway.
"full of laughs and full of lovers."
Ernest Hemingway Collection. John F. Kennedy Presidential Library and Museum, Boston, Massachusetts.

ONCE BACK IN EUROPE, ERNEST CONTINUED HIS PURSUIT OF NEW adventures in new places with new people. The success of *For Whom the Bell Tolls* and the articles he had written for the North American Newspaper Alliance during the Spanish Civil War gave him a voice of authority and new leverage as a war correspondent. He sought assignments that allowed him to cover some of the hardest fought and bloodiest battles of 1944 and 1945, and he placed himself in dangerous situations to be part of the action and absorb the experiences needed for a good story. Along the way, he met new people and soon discovered the woman who would become his fourth wife.

After the D-Day invasion, he set up headquarters at the Hotel du Grand Veneur in Rambouillet outside of Paris. War correspondents were not allowed to bear arms or participate in military action, but Ernest convinced Colonel David Bruce to give him authorization to participate in military intelligence activities. The Germans were approaching, and the consensus was they would take the town of Rambouillet. Ernest took over intelligence operations regarding German activity on the road to Paris. Using English, French, and broken German, he interrogated German deserters and prisoners as they were captured and collected information regarding roadblocks, radar installations, and anti-aircraft defenses between Rambouillet and Paris. His take-charge attitude and actions annoyed other war correspondents, but David Bruce, the Office of Strategic Services officer who authorized his position at Rambouillet, later said:

> I entertain a great admiration for [Ernest] not only as an artist and friend, but as a cool, resourceful, imaginative military tactician and strategist. He unites, from what I saw of him, that rare combination of advised recklessness and caution that knows how to properly seize upon a favorable opportunity which, once lost, is gone forever. He was a born leader of men, and in spite of his strong independence of character, impressed me as a highly disciplined individual.[1]

When Paris was liberated, Ernest didn't march down the Champs-Élysées but instead went straight to the bar at the Paris Ritz and ordered champagne for everyone.

Though Ernest and Martha were still married, Ernest's new interest was Mary Welsh Monks, a feature writer for *Time* who was married to Australian journalist Noel Monks. Irwin Shaw had introduced Ernest to Mary in London before D-Day. Mary was having lunch with Shaw in the White Tower restaurant in London and attracting attention, braless under a summer sweater. Their clipped conversation indicates Ernest's immediate attraction to her.

"Nice sweater."

"Warmth does bring things out."

"Shaw, introduce me to your friend."[2]

That evening, Ernest went to Mary's room in the Dorchester Hotel and told her, "I don't know you, Mary. But I want to marry you. You are very alive. You're beautiful. Like a May fly."[3] She was silent, but he continued, "I want to marry you now, and I hope to marry you sometime. Sometime you may want to marry me."[4] Mary replied that he was being silly and reminded him that they were both married, but he still continued, "Just please remember I want to marry you. Now and tomorrow and next month and next year."[5] After he left, Mary thought he was probably just lonesome and concluded he was just too big—both in stature and status.

Both Ernest and Mary were in failing marriages. After D-Day, Martha left Ernest, and Mary, believing she was a better reporter than her husband, began to find him dull. When Paris was liberated, Ernest checked into the Paris Ritz, and conveniently Mary checked in the next day. She was confident with men, and if one flirted with her, she was ready. Her colleague at Time-Life, Bill Walton, saw Mary as being "full of laughs and full of lovers."[6]

Their introduction soon turned into a physical relationship, but both Ernest and Mary continued as war correspondents until the end of the war. Ernest covered battles along the Belgian border and the Siegfried Line. He joined Colonel Charles "Buck" Lanham during the 1944 Battle of Hurtgenwald, in which thousands of Americans were killed, wounded, or demoralized by the piercing cold and winter rains that turned the battlefields into seas of mud. Though Lanham was a writer and poet as well as a West Point graduate, it was the hard battles and horrendous conditions that cemented his friendship with Ernest.

Figure 6.2. Ernest Hemingway with Colonel "Buck" Lanham Schweitzer, Germany, during World War II. *Ernest Hemingway Collection. John F. Kennedy Presidential Library and Museum, Boston, Massachusetts.*

The Allied goal at Hurtgenwald was to contain German forces in the area to keep them from reinforcing the frontlines farther north, where the US forces were fighting against the Siegfried Line. However, the Germans had filled the area with minefields, barbed wire, and booby traps, and the dense forest allowed German infiltration and flanking attacks. The wet, cloudy weather hindered Allied air support; the dense forest and rough terrain prevented movement of Allied tanks and trucks.

Ernest walked through flooded fields, waist high mud, and heaps of German dead to get experiences and firsthand information for his articles for *Collier's*, but Mary also was on his mind. Given the harrowing conditions and the life-threatening experiences, he made Mary the sole beneficiary of his *Collier's* wartime insurance policy. When he was able to write to her, he asked her to "Please love me very much and always take care of me Small Friend the way Small Friends take care of Big Friends. . . . Oh Mary darling I love you very much."[7] Later, he also asked her to consider a future life with him in Cuba. He told her to "think about the boat and the dark blue, almost purple of the Gulf Stream . . . and us on the flying bridge steering in shorts and no tops and at night anchored behind the barrier reef down at Paraiso with the sea pounding on the lovely sand."[8]

When Ernest returned to Paris from the Battle of Hurtgenwald, he had severe pneumonia, and Lanham ordered the regimental doctor to treat him with massive doses of sulfa. After he recovered, he continued to visit battle sectors, but told Patrick "after this one I'm going to Cuba, fix up the grounds . . . write a book."[9] As the Allied victory approached, Mary, who had been writing about conditions in France and Germany for the Time, Inc. radio series, *March of Time*, asked her boss for an indefinite leave of absence and told Ernest she would try living in Cuba. In April 1945, Ernest returned to the Finca and in May Mary arrived in Havana.

Having thought about his three previous marriages, Ernest used his experiences to filter and judge the essential criteria for the woman who would become his fourth wife. He deduced that he did not want a professional rival such as Martha, but rather someone with the support and stability of Hadley and the household skills of Pauline.

While they were at the Paris Ritz, Mary had found a letter from Ernest to Pauline and learned that Pauline "ran a shipshape gracious

Figure 6.3. Ernest and Mary Hemingway's wedding photo in Havana, Cuba, March 14, 1946.
Keystone-France/Getty Images

house in Key West," but that he planned to marry Mary because she was "sensible and reliable, and that [she] would look after him and the children."[10] After reading the letter, Mary concluded that she would need to give up her career and accept the fact that Ernest wanted a "practical nurse" for himself and his children.[11] Mary accepted the challenge, and their divorces proceeded without contest. Mary went from Mrs. Monks to Miss Welsh on August 31, 1945, and Ernest was divorced from Martha on grounds of her desertion of him on December 21, 1945. On March 13, 1946, Ernest and Mary were married in Havana.

Mary's life quickly changed:

> Ernest, the Finc Vigia, and Cuba Bella presented [her with] a variety of challenges: a new language, a new climate, a world of blossoms on trees, vines, shrubs and stalks [she] didn't know, a large staff and so a new manner of living, new diversions requiring new skills—fishing and shooting—a one-leader boss of operations instead of the complex hierarchy of Time Inc., and new focus of interest and activity. No office. [She] had an entire new life to learn, and [she] was glad that [she] had decided, leaving Europe, that [she] would refrain from trying to keep close ties by regular correspondence with [her] friends there. A sharp break, but neat.[12]

Upon arriving in Cuba, Mary took Spanish lessons and worked toward being a good wife and manager of a complicated household. The house and guest house were set on fifteen acres that contained flower and vegetable gardens, fruit trees, eighteen different kinds of mangoes, and a variety of trees that supported orchids. In addition, there was a swimming pool and a tennis court. The "charming ruin" of the house contained a fifty-foot living room, a dining room, library, guest bedroom and master bedroom, as well as a wing that housed a study, bedroom, and bathroom, where Ernest wrote. Later, Mary also built a tower as a quiet place where Ernest could work.

Mary erased the artifacts of Martha's presence, made some architectural changes to the house, and over time filled the Finca with Ernest's favorite things. In addition to comfortable furniture, designed by Mary and handmade in Cuba, the house was populated with horned animal

Figure 6.4. Jack (Bumby) and Patrick in the living room at Finca Vigia, San Francisco de Paula, Cuba.
Ernest Hemingway Collection. John F. Kennedy Presidential Library and Museum, Boston, Massachusetts.

trophies in almost every room. The library contained five thousand books, but there also were books in the bedrooms, his study, and his bathroom and a large magazine rack packed with American and foreign magazines and newspapers. The Finca became a comfortable setting for Ernest to write, as well as a home to entertain friends and family. Mary also hoped to increase the size of the family by having the baby girl Ernest always wanted, but she was heartbroken when she lost her baby due to a life-threatening ectopic pregnancy.

Despite disappointments and challenges, Mary became an accomplished cook and hostess. She learned to share Ernest's enthusiasm for hunting, fishing, and spending days at a time aboard the *Pilar*, and welcomed Ernest's friends, who came from a broad range of backgrounds and interests. She entertained refugees from the Spanish Civil War, fishermen and boat captains Ernest met on the docks, as well as Hollywood stars who appeared in the film versions of his books. Dinner regulars included Roberto Herrera, who came to Cuba after being

Figure 6.5. Adeline Beehler Welsh, Mary Hemingway, Juan "Sinsky" Dunabeitia, Ernest Hemingway, and Gianfranco Ivancich dining at Finca Vigia, San Francisco de Paula, Cuba.
Ernest Hemingway Collection. John F. Kennedy Presidential Library and Museum, Boston, Massachusetts.

imprisoned for fighting on the Loyalist side in the Spanish Civil War, Sinsky Dunabeitia, a Basque boat captain who manned a freighter that ran between the United States and Cuba, and Father Don Andres, whom Ernest called "Black Priest." Like Herrera, Father Andres had fought in the Spanish Civil War, first advising his parishioners to grab their guns and fight rather than spending time in church and then serving as a machine gunner for the Loyalist army.

In an interview for *Look* magazine, Ernest summarized his new wife's virtues, saying, "Miss Mary is durable. She is also brave, charming, witty, exciting to look at, a pleasure to be with and a good wife. She is an

Figure 6.6. The Hemingways at La Florida ("Floridita"), Havana, Cuba.

L–R: Roberto Hererra, unidentified man, Gianfranco Ivancich, Mary Hemingway, Dora Ivancich, Ernest Hemingway, and Adriana Ivancich.

Ernest Hemingway Collection. John F. Kennedy Presidential Library and Museum, Boston.

excellent fisherwoman, a fair wing shot, a strong swimmer, a really good cook, and good judge of wine, and excellent gardener . . . and can run a boat or a household in Spanish."[13]

When Mary gave up her career to take care of Ernest and his household, her life changed. Running the household at Finca Vigía was no small task, and she was compelled to embrace a set of salty characters Ernest considered friends. When their mutual friend, Irwin Shaw, published his book *The Young Lions*, the change became even more obvious. Shaw's character, Louise, was a thinly veiled picture of Mary: Louise was a woman with a "small, elegant body, [who] seemed to know every bigwig in the British Isles. She had a deft, tricky way with men, and was always being invited to weekends at famous country houses were garrulous military men of high rank seemed to spill a great many dangerous secrets to her."[14]

Shaw assumed that after the war "[Louise] would run for the Senate or be appointed as an Ambassadress to somewhere."[15] But, rather than becoming an "ambassadress to somewhere" like Louise, Mary started to endure a life that was frequently punctuated with periods of humiliation, embarrassment, and sometimes fear.

In October 1948, Ernest and Mary returned to Italy, planning to spend the fall in Venice and the winter in Cortina'd Ampezzo. During the fall while hunting for ducks at Baron Nanyuki Franchetti's lodge north of Venice, Ernest met the Ivancich family and became absolutely captivated by their eighteen-year-old daughter, Adriana. He admired her for braving the rain while duck hunting but was more taken with her when he saw her drying her long dark hair in front of the fireplace at the hunting lodge. Learning that she had no comb, he broke his in two and gave her half. Though Adriana was beautiful, her age, her devout Catholicism, and her membership in an aristocratic Venetian family that was highly conscious of Venetian proprieties made her an unlikely match for the married, forty-nine-year-old author. However, Adriana was flattered by Ernest's attention and intrigued with her friendship with the famous author. They saw each other every day during the 1948 visit to Venice, lunching at the Gritti Palace Hotel, drinking at Harry's Bar, and strolling along the canals of Venice. They even skied together in Cortina.

After Mary broke her ankle skiing and Ernest contracted an eye infection that sent him to the hospital in Padua for ten days, Mary and

Ernest returned to the Finca. However, after several years of intense correspondence, Adriana, her brother, Gianfranco, and her mother were invited to visit Finca Vigia in 1950. Ernest continued to be infatuated with Adriana, and during her visit, he behaved erratically and emotionally. Given his interest in Adriana, he tried to precipitate a break with Mary. Ernest didn't like it when Gianfranco introduced Adriana to his younger friends, and when Mary offered to type a visa application for Gianfranco so he could accompany Ernest, Mary, and Adriana on a trip to the United States, Ernest became enraged and threw her typewriter on the floor. Later that evening, when Mary tried to cajole him into a better mood by dancing with him, he threw a glass of wine at her. However, despite his humiliating actions and comments, Mary stayed the course, saying, "No matter what you say or do . . . I'm going to stay here and run your house and your Finca."[16]

Again, writing from his personal experience, Ernest used Adriana as the model for the character, Renata, in his next novel, *Across the River and Into the Trees*. Renata, like Adriana, was from an aristocratic Venetian family and had lost both her father and her ancestral villa to the violence of World War II. The plot of the novel centers on the comfort and renewal the fifty-year-old Colonel Cantwell finds in his love for the nineteen-year-old Renata and his determination to experience her love of life and youthful sense of immortality until the very end. After spending three days in Venice enjoying food and drink and making love to Renata, Cantwell, foreshadowing his own death, quotes the final words of Stonewall Jackson, "Let's go across the river and rest in the shade of the trees."[17] He then makes his way to the backseat of the staff car and dies of a heart attack.

The plot of the novel was fueled by the intensity of emotion Ernest felt for Adriana, and his belief that the formula of love and war which had been so successful in *A Farewell to Arms* and *For Whom the Bell Tolls* would work in *Across the River and Into the Trees*. Ernest modeled the character of Colonel Cantwell after himself. Cantwell is a fifty-year-old American officer, a veteran of two world wars, an observer in the Spanish Civil War, and separated from his ambitious wife, who is a war correspondent.

Having fought in the Battle of Hurtgenwald, the colonel describes to Renata the details of the conflict. On the battlefield, "There was snow, or something, rain or fog all the time and the roads had been mined as many as fourteen mines deep in certain stretches, so when the vehicles churned down to a new string deeper, in another part of the mud, you were always losing vehicles and, of course, the people that went with them."[18] Then he gives the grim details of the German dead: "In Hurtgen they just froze up hard; and it was so cold they froze up with ruddy faces. Very strange. They all were gray and yellow like wax-works in the summer. But once the winter came they had ruddy faces."[19]

When Renata asks the colonel about his marriage, he says, "She was an ambitious woman and I was away too much." He explains, "She had more ambition than Napoleon and about the talent of the average High School Valedictorian."[20] When Renata suggests they forget about her, the colonel reassures her that "she is gone away, for good and forever; cauterized; exorcised and with the eleven copies of her reclassification papers, in which was included the formal, notarized act of divorcement, in triplicate."[21] The description of the ex-wife was so obviously linked to Martha that Ernest's publisher thought the reference might be libelous. Ernest's retort, however, was that Martha shouldn't consider trading punches with him.

Renata's dialog and questions are those of a young, inexperienced woman. Like Adriana, Renata is a graduate of a Catholic girls' school and a sheltered member of an aristocratic Venetian family. She also is beautiful, and her long dark hair is an important detail in her physical description. Arriving at the Gritti Palace Hotel, "she came into the room, shining in her youth and tall striding beauty, and the carelessness the wind had made of her hair. She had pale, almost olive colored skin a profile that could break your, or any one else's heart, and her dark hair, of an alive texture, hung down over her shoulders."[22]

Hoping for another bestseller, Ernest continued to take literary risks in the novel, and the characters' heroic lovemaking under a blanket onboard a gondola made the book famous. The aging colonel is told to "attack gently."[23] Then, unlike Adriana, the lusty young Renata requests, "Let's do it again, please."[24] Cantwell's passion and lovemaking with

Renata is clearly drawn from Ernest's infatuation with Adriana, but their "love story" was as improbable and unrealistic to the reader as Ernest's May-September love for Adriana was to his wife and friends. Everyone, except Ernest, saw Ernest's infatuation with Adriana as an embarrassing midlife folly of an aging writer.

Though Adriana was attracted to Ernest because he told her that she restored energy to his writing, she did not feel the same intensity of affection as he did. After the publication of the book, Ernest, Charles Scribner, Mary, and Adriana had lunch in Paris. After lunch, Ernest and Adriana went for a walk and stopped at the literary café Deux Magots. Ernest told Adriana that any of the men, if they saw her and were not stupid, would want to marry her.

"Since I am not stupid, I would feel the same way."

"But you have Mary," said Adriana.

"Ah, yes, Mary. She is nice of course, and solid and courageous."[25]

During their conversation, Ernest explained that a couple could travel a part of a road together and then take two different directions and that it had already happened to him. He promised Adriana that it would not happen to them and told her, "I love you in my heart and I cannot do anything about it."[26]

He continued, "I know what you need to be happy. I will live to make you happy," and then said, "I would ask you to marry me, if I didn't know that you would say no."[27]

Adrian stood up and they walked along the Seine. Adriana later told friends, "I appreciated his kindnesses and his attention. We were friends."[28]

No one but Ernest approved of the new book. Adriana believed, "A girl like that does not exist, if she is lovely and from a good family and goes to Mass every morning. Such a girl would not drink all day like a sponge and be in bed at the hotel."[29] Mary found the conversations between Colonel Cantwell and his girl "banal beyond reason."[30] The critics agreed. Maxwell Geismar said in the *Saturday Review of Literature* that not only was *Across the River and Into the Trees* Ernest's "worst novel [but] a synthesis of everything that is bad in his previous work."[31] J. Donald Adams, writing for *The New York Times*, described it as "one of the saddest books I have ever read; not because I am moved to compassion by the conjunction of love and death in the Colonel's life, but because a great talent has come, whether for now or forever, to such a dead end."[32]

Ernest, however, was convinced he had written another masterpiece. After Mary read part of the manuscript, he told Charlie Scribner that Mary "waits on me hand and foot and doesn't give a damn if I have whores or countesses or what as long as I have the luck to write like that."[33] Then he countered the attacks of the critics, saying, "Sure, they can say anything about nothing happening in *Across the River*, but all that happens is the defense of the lower Piave, the breakthrough in Normandy, the taking of Paris and the destruction of the 22nd Infantry in Hurtgen Forest plus a man who loves a girl and dies."[34] He hoped that the risk-taking that propelled him to early fame would bolster the reviews and made a case for himself as an experimental writer, saying, "I have moved through arithmetic, through plane geometry and algebra, and now I am in in calculus. If they don't understand that, to hell with them."[35]

Ernest's interlude with Adriana was consistent with his pattern of escaping the routine of married life. No matter how good his life was with Hadley or Pauline, he left for a new adventure with a new woman. The differences in the situation with Adriana were she was not interested in Ernest as a romantic partner, and Mary refused to leave him despite his behavior. Though the Ivancich family valued Ernest's friendship, his use of Adriana as the model for Renata made it difficult for any of them to live a normal life in Venice. Adriana experienced a new sort of popularity as "Hemingway's girlfriend," but Adriana, her mother, and her brothers were embarrassed by the snickering and rumors that accompanied the reading of *Across the River and Into the Trees*. Though Ernest had forbade the Italian publication of the book for at least two years and wrote a letter to Adriana testifying that she was not the girl in the book, Adriana and her family continued to be surrounded by painful gossip.

After writing his final letter to Adriana, Ernest settled down in Cuba and focused on rescuing his reputation as a writer. Because he had used specific personal experiences as the content for many successful short stories and novels, his critics claimed he could write about nothing except himself and his own experiences. Assuming the criticism was valid, Ernest began developing a character that was not as personally connected with himself as Fredric Henry, Robert Jordan, and Colonel Cantwell had been. The new character was an old fisherman, one he knew from the harbor at Cojimar.

The plot follows Santiago, the old fisherman, who has not caught a fish in eighty-four days. His village considers him *salao* (unlucky), and his boy, Manolin, has been forced by his parents to work on a different, luckier boat. On the eighty-fifth day of his losing streak, Santiago takes his skiff out early, intending to row far into the Gulf Stream. He catches a small albacore in the morning, then hooks a huge marlin. The fish is too heavy to haul in and begins to tow the skiff further out to sea. Santiago holds on through the night. The sunset arrives for a second time and on the third morning the marlin begins to circle. Santiago draws the marlin in and harpoons it and lashes it to the skiff. Smelling the blood in the water, sharks attack. Santiago kills the first shark but loses his harpoon. Next, he lashes his knife to an oar as a makeshift spear and kills three more sharks before the knife blade snaps. He clubs two more sharks at sunset, but on the third night, the sharks come as a pack and leave only bones of the fish behind them.

When Santiago returns to shore, he sleeps in his shack, leaving the skeleton tied to his skiff. Manolin cries when he sees Santiago's situation but brings him coffee and insists on accompanying him in the future. The story ends as Santiago goes back to sleep and dreams of lions on an African beach.

While the old man's loss was not personally experienced by Ernest, the character's unsuccessful efforts in bringing in the marlin reflect Ernest's own unsuccessful experiences with the politely indifferent Adriana and the unsuccessful reception to *Across the River and Into the Trees*. Like Santiago, Ernest may have ventured too far from shore on the Gulf Stream of his risk-taking literary career and been attacked by shark-like critics. And, like the old man, who had been a champion arm wrestler and a successful fisherman, Ernest, too, was trying for a comeback.

Though Ernest was not the old man, his fishing experiences contributed to the book. He knew well the inhabitants of the Gulf Stream and the pattern of one, then two, then more sharks attacking a valuable catch as well as the sensation of killing a shark by driving a knife blade

Figure 6.7. Ernest Hemingway in the cabin of his boat, *Pilar*.
Ernest Hemingway Collection. John F. Kennedy Presidential Library and Museum, Boston, Massachusetts.

between its vertebrae and brain. He knew, too, the details of the old man's skiff and what he would have had on board and the order he would use the items to counter the attack of sharks—first a harpoon, then a knife lashed to the butt of an oar, and finally the tiller and rudder. Ernest made use of his twenty years' experience on the Gulf. "[He] knew about a man in that situation with a fish. [He] knew what happened in a boat, in a sea, fighting a fish. So [he] took a man [he] knew for twenty years and imagined him under those circumstances."[36]

The old man also embraces the code for living that Ernest first developed after his experiences in World War I—the experiences in which a man confronts an unconquerable element. This time it wasn't man confronting the circumstances of war and almost certain death, but man confronting sharks and almost certain death. The old man exhibits courage and grace under pressure. Like Ernest, he understands the reality of facing death, but fights the sharks, believing "a man can be destroyed, but not defeated."[37]

Mary was captivated by Ernest's literary genius and despite their domestic conflicts, continued to care for and support him. As Ernest wrote, Mary read the story of the old man each night from beginning to end. The story gave her goose bumps, but as the end approached, she sensed something more than the tragedy of the fish. When she asked if the old man was going to die, Ernest's reply was, "Maybe better for him."[38] She argued for herself and others that, "everybody would be happier if you let him live"[39] and was relieved when she read the last lines of the story. "Up the road, in his shack, the old man was sleeping again. He was still sleeping on his face and the boy was sitting by him watching him. The old man was dreaming about the lions."[40]

Though Ernest doesn't tell the reader whether the old man is going to live or die, Mary, as well as future readers and critics, believed Santiago's dream about the lions was a victory over the village's prejudice that he was finished as a fisherman. Though Ernest foreshadowed the possibility of death, Mary, like others, wanted to believe that his dream was a joyful symbol of his ability to conquer defeat. Santiago comes to terms with the present, but by remembering the lions, he does not let go of his past and the experiences that made him the man he is. Mary's hope for

Figure 6.8. Ernest and Mary Hemingway on safari in Africa, 1953–1954. *Ernest Hemingway Collection. John F. Kennedy Presidential Library and Museum, Boston, Massachusetts.*

the old man was her hope for Ernest—that he was not ready to let go of his past and that he also had come to terms with his present.

The idea that man can be destroyed but not defeated sent a message of hope to the world, and the reviews and success of *The Old Man and the Sea* were nothing less than phenomenal. The *New Republic* called Ernest "unquestionably the greatest craftsman of the American novel in this century."[41] *The New York Times* claimed, "Here is the master technician once more at the top of his form, doing superbly what he can do better than anyone else."[42] Appropriately, Ernest was aboard the *Pilar* and out on the Gulf Stream when he heard via the ship's radio that the book had been awarded the Pulitzer Prize. Advance sales of the Scribner's publication

Figure 6.9. Ernest and Mary Hemingway with a water buffalo on safari in Africa, 1953–1954.
Ernest Hemingway Collection. John F. Kennedy Presidential Library and Museum, Boston, Massachusetts.

ran to fifty thousand with more weekly sales of three thousand copies thereafter. Because of the simplicity of style and the universality of its theme, the book was translated into numerous languages. In addition to US and foreign royalties, Ernest sold the film rights for $150,000.

Having regained his reputation as the greatest craftsman of the American novel, Ernest and Mary celebrated by heading to Franco's Spain for bullfights in Pamplona and then to Africa to engage in another safari. Mary followed in the footsteps of Ernest's three previous wives with enthusiasm and fortitude. In Pamplona, she engaged in the sights and festivities Hadley and Pauline once enjoyed. Attending the

Figure 6.10. Wreckage of the Cessna 180 plane that carried Ernest and Mary Hemingway, near Murchison Falls, Uganda. Ernest Hemingway Collection. *John F. Kennedy Presidential Library and Museum, Boston, Massachusetts.*

obligatory bullfights, she wrote in her diary that Antonio Ordonez "did the most brilliant passes . . . slow and sure . . . he was luminous between the great horns and the bull died bravely."[43] Later in Madrid, she and Ernest stayed at the Hotel Florida where Ernest had lived with Martha during the Spanish Civil War, and apparently, Mary shared Ernest's view that "there were no ghosts."[44]

Leaving Spain, they boarded a ship in Marseilles and headed to Mombassa. Ernest, Mary, and their guide, Philip Percival, began the safari south of Nairobi and looked forward to hunting lions and leopards. Ernest shot his first lion soon after they arrived, and, after time and a lot of practice, Mary shot a male lion in his right leg and a guide followed, breaking the lion's spine with a larger bullet.

Sleeping in a tent, pursuing wildlife, and drinking gin in front of the fire after a day of hunting was an aphrodisiac for Mary. She reported in her diary that their lovemaking was "little private carnivals."[45] However, happy as they may have been in the privacy of their tent, Ernest didn't hesitate to go native and shave his head, carry a spear, and select a native fiancée. Mary acknowledged the infidelity by suggesting that Debba first take a much-needed bath. Then Ernest invited Debba and several of her friends to his tent when Mary flew to Nairobi for shopping.

Though Ernest's celebration with the native women caused his cot to collapse, Mary continued to remain cheerful and enthusiastic about the trip. As a gift to Mary, Ernest chartered a small Cessna 180 for the purpose of sight-seeing in the Belgian Congo. After seeing herds of hippopotamus, elephants, and buffaloes, they flew over the Ngorongoro Center so that Mary could see where Pauline had killed her lion in 1933. However, as they flew over Murchison Falls and headed toward Entebbe, the plane encountered a large flock of birds. Trying to avoid a collision, the pilot struck a telegraph wire and the plane crashed into low trees and heavy brush. Though Mary, Ernest, and the pilot were all injured, they survived the crash. After spending the night above a crocodile-infested river, Ernest sighted a boat, which they were able to take to Butiaba.

There, they boarded a de Havilland Rapide hoping to head back to Entebbe, where reporters were waiting to learn whether the rumors that Ernest had been killed were true.

Figure 6.11. Ernest and Mary Hemingway's house in Ketchum, Idaho. *N. Sindelar Collection.*

Shortly after takeoff, the de Havilland Rapide crashed and began to burn. Mary and the pilot escaped by kicking out a window. Ernest tried to escape through a door that turned out to be jammed. As the cabin burned, he used his dislocated shoulder and his head to finally open the door and exited onto the lower left wing of the biplane. When fully examined, he learned he not only had a dislocated shoulder, but also had another concussion, two cracked discs in his spine, and ruptures in his liver and one of his kidneys.

After thirteen months of travel, they returned to the Finca, and Ernest's moods became increasing irritable. He ached from his injuries

Figure 6.12. Ernest and Mary Hemingway at La Consula, Malaga, Spain, 1959. L–R: Nathan "Bill" Davis, Rupert Bellville, Ernest Hemingway, Mary Hemingway, Juan Quintana.
Ernest Hemingway Collection. John F. Kennedy Presidential Library and Museum, Boston, Massachusetts.

and was besieged by guests, curious tourists, and movie people. Ernest was involved in making *The Old Man and the Sea* into a movie, Scribner's was eager to publish his Paris memoirs, and Ernest and A. E. Hotchner had formed a lucrative partnership for television programming based on Ernest's short stories and novels. Unlike the early years, he was making a lot of money—for himself, his publishers, and his producers. However, his body was deteriorating, and his moods were increasingly irrational. He not only had two skull fractures and at least seven concussions and other subconcussive head traumas, but he also had developed an enlarged liver due to heavy use of alcohol and skin cancer due to many hours in the sun.

When he learned he had been awarded the Nobel Prize on October 28, 1954, he accepted the award but chose not to attend the ceremony in Stockholm. Rather, he sent a written statement that was read by John Cabot, the American ambassador to Sweden. Though he was at the height of a distinguished literary career and had received the impressive award, his statement is laced with his feelings of loneliness and a sense of decline. Ernest tells his audience that, "Writing, at its best, is a lonely life. Organizations for writers palliate the writer's loneliness but I doubt if they improve his writing. He grows in public stature as he sheds his loneliness and often his work deteriorates. For he does his work alone and if he is a good enough writer he must face eternity, or the lack of it, each day."[46]

In addition to his physical irritations, Ernest saw the signs of revolution brewing in Cuba. The Batista regime was being challenged by Fidel Castro. Ernest did not support Batista and hoped that Castro would just leave Mary and him alone. When Castro won the Hemingway Fishing Tournament, Ernest presented him with the trophy, but the pressure to leave Cuba mounted when the Castro regime began vilifying the United States. Then, one night a Batista search party tried to enter the Finca, looking for guns. One of the soldiers clubbed to death Ernest's favorite dog, Black Dog, using the butt of his rifle. Knowing the atrocities that occurred in Spain during the Spanish Civil War, Ernest decided it was time to purchase a house in Idaho. Ernest told Patrick:

> Cuba is really bad now, Mouse. I am not a big fear danger pussy but living in a country where no one is right—both sides atrocious—knowing what sort of stuff and murder will go on when the new ones come

in—seeing the abuses of those in now—I am fed on it. We are always treated OK as in all countries and have fine good friends. But things aren't good . . . Might pull out.[47]

Ernest and Mary decided to "pull out" of Cuba in April 1959 and moved to a house about a mile from the Sun Valley resort in the town of Ketchum. The square, rather fortress-like house was built on a hillside overlooking the Big Wood River and had large picture windows with a view of the Sawtooth Mountains. The refuge was purchased from the millionaire sportsman Bob Topping for fifty thousand dollars. Set on seventeen acres of aspens and cottonwood trees, the location offered privacy and the back bedroom was identified as an ideal study for Ernest. The large kitchen had modern appliances, and Mary soon hosted dinners of roasted duck and pheasant for friends and hunting companions.

By the time Ernest lived in the Ketchum house, his ailments from various injuries; the pressures for more articles, short stories, and novels; and the political complications of being a US citizen with a house in Cuba had begun to take their toll. However, when Ernest's Idaho friend, Bill Davis, invited Ernest and Mary to his estate in the Costa del Sol of southern Spain, Ernest was excited to pursue a new adventure, and Mary cooperated. Their plan was to attend a series of bullfights, including a *mano a mano*, in which two matadors alternate competing for the admiration of the audience. They especially looked forward to an extraordinary contest between Antonio Ordonez and Luis Miguel Dominguin.

During the trip, Mary organized a sixtieth birthday party for Ernest at La Consula, the Davis's estate. The extravaganza included flamenco dancers, target-shooting booths, and fireworks. The champagne came from Paris, and Mary prepared a special sweet and sour sauce for the turkey entree. Friends came from all over Europe and the United States, including Buck Lanham, David and Evangeline Bruce, Gianfranco Ivancich and his wife, and Ernest's Sun Valley doctor, Geoge Saviers and his wife. Mary had tried to create a truly special and memorable event for Ernest, but he was nasty and accused her of spending all his money. There was a fight, and Mary threatened to leave Ernest and get an apartment in New York. Then came a make-up period that included a new diamond pin.

In addition to spending time at the Davises' estate and attending a season of bullfights, *Life* had contacted Ernest to write an article on bullfighting. When the bullfight season concluded, Ernest returned to Cuba to work on the article, then went back to Spain to check facts and collect photographs. In Spain, he worked feverishly on the article, titled "Dangerous Summer." He also wrote foreboding letters from Spain to Mary in Cuba, saying "I wish you were here to look after me and help me out and keep [me] from cracking up."[48] He became increasingly moody and irrational. Writing became a struggle, his daily routine was destroyed along with his self-confidence, and his creativity was replaced by anxiety. Ernest spent months agonizing over details that he felt were so important to the total effect of the story. Given his struggle, the managing editor of *Life* eventually made cuts to create a forty-thousand-word article, and Scribner's agreed to do a full-length book version of 130,000 words, also called *The Dangerous Summer.*

Though Ernest's ability to make new friends survived his move to Sun Valley, his desire to be with people waned. Moody and depressed, he wanted to be alone. However, despite his mood swings and frequent verbal attacks, Mary honored the commitment that she understood would be necessary when they first courted in Paris. She continued to accept the fact that Ernest wanted, and now needed, a "practical nurse." As she witnessed his decline, she believed his personality changed. She said he was "almost the opposite of what he had been before—outgoing and exuberant and articulate and full of life."[49] Now he was "all inward and quiet and inarticulate."[50]

In addition to the anxiety created by not being able to write, Ernest believed he was being followed by the Federal Bureau of Investigation (FBI). He was suspicious of strangers in restaurants and males in topcoats. Driving home one night, he saw lights on the second floor of their bank in Ketchum. Though his wife and friends in the car thought the lights were on for the bank's cleaning crew, Ernest was convinced the FBI was investigating his bank accounts. Paranoia was taking control of his life, but his suspicions were not unfounded. The FBI had opened a file on him at the time of his Crook Factory operation in Cuba in the 1940s, and agents reported regularly on his activities for the rest of his life.

When Ernest returned to Cuba from Spain in 1959, he expressed his support for Castro to reporters, saying, "I am very happy to be here again because I consider myself a Cuban. I have not believed any of the reports against Cuba. I sympathize with the Cuban government and with all our difficulties."[51] Then he kissed the hem of the Cuban flag. When reporters asked him to repeat the act for a photograph, he refused. Kissing the Cuban flag had been a genuine expression of his love of Cuba and the Cuban people, but he was nervous about repeating it. Though Ernest did not embrace Communism and believed Batista "looted (Cuba) naked when he left," Ernest was conflicted about showing his support for Cuba and its people once Castro was in power.[52] His apprehension was well founded as both his statement and his act of kissing the Cuban flag were carefully documented in his FBI file.

Given Ernest's heightened levels of depression and anxiety, his Idaho doctor, George Saviers, suggested psychiatric treatment. Though Ernest initially was concerned about negative publicity and said, "They'll say I'm losing my marbles," Mary supported the plan and he registered at the Mayo Clinic in Rochester, Minnesota, under an assumed name.[53] The doctors took him off his blood pressure medicine, which they believed caused depression, and recommended electric shock therapy twice a week. Between November 1960 and January 1961, Ernest began electro-shock treatment. A rubber gag was placed in his mouth, electrodes were placed on his head, and an electric current was sent to his brain. Each of the electro-shock treatments produced a grand mal seizure, the equivalent of a concussion. Each time Ernest awoke, he was in a coma-like state, unable to say where he was or why. His memories and experiences were lost, and he felt a sense of despair and futility when he could only vaguely sense the past. Since his memories of places, people, and events were the substance of his writing and the source of his success as a writer, the loss of memory was a catastrophic event. After the first round of treatments, Ernest returned to the house in Ketchum. He tried to work on the Paris book, *A Moveable Feast*, and out of habit told Mary he was "working hard," but he couldn't write, and his depression increased.

When Ernest learned of the April 1961 Bay of Pigs disaster and the failure of the Central Intelligence Agency to trigger an uprising against the pro-Communist Castro regime, Ernest knew he would not be returning to Cuba. He suspected he would never see his Finca, the *Pilar*, his collection of modernist paintings, his five-thousand-volume library, or his unpublished manuscripts again, and he was right. After the Bay of Pigs, the Castro government appropriated the Finca, and Ernest never returned.

Given his preoccupation with the eventuality of death and how man faced it, Ernest had already considered his own end. He believed suicide was a common-sense way for many people to end their lives. He told others exactly how he would execute his own suicide, once saying to Martha that one could place the barrel of a shotgun on one's head and discharge a full blast through the barrel by placing one's toe on the trigger and bearing down.

Six days after the failed Cuban invasion, Mary found Ernest in the vestibule of their house, holding a shotgun and two shells. She talked with him for over an hour, until Dr. Saviers arrived and took him to the Sun Valley Hospital. After a few days in the hospital, Ernest talked his doctor into letting him go home. When he arrived at the house, he bolted out of the car, went into the house, found his shotgun, and began loading it with shells. Their neighbor, Don Anderson, saw what was happening and was able to wrestle the gun away. Ernest was taken back to the Sun Valley Hospital, and the next day Ernest and Mary flew in a friend's plane to the Mayo Clinic. When the plane was being refueled in Rapid City, South Dakota, Ernest headed straight for the whirling propeller of another airplane, which stopped only after the pilot cut the engine.

Arriving at the Mayo Clinic, Ernest endured more electric shock treatments. Then he followed the doctor's orders and took daily walks, swam, and practiced target shooting. Though the shock treatments continued, Ernest eventually convinced the doctor that he was better and could go home again. He charmed the doctor and promised he would not attempt suicide. When Mary arrived at the doctor's office, she was "dumbfounded to see Ernest there, dressed in his street clothes, grinning like a Cheshire cat."[54]

Mary was convinced Ernest had tricked the doctor into thinking he was okay but didn't argue. They headed back to Ketchum by car and arrived on June 30. The next night they dined with friends at the local

Christiana Inn. Ernest was distracted by men he thought were FBI agents, but after a pleasant dinner, he and Mary went home and slept in their separate bedrooms.

The next morning, July 2, 1961, Ernest rose before seven, left his back bedroom, and took the keys to unlock the basement door. There he picked out his double-barreled Boss shotgun from the rack and went to the upstairs vestibule. Though he could no longer write, he still remembered the skill he had learned from his father, the skill he practiced in the woods of Michigan, in the green hills of Africa, and in the mountains of Idaho. He slipped two cartridges into the barrels of the gun, lowered the gun butt to the floor, pressed his forehead against the barrels, and blew away his entire cranial vault.

Mary awoke in the comfortable round bed in the master bedroom on the upper level of the house. She thought she had heard two drawers being slammed shut and went downstairs to investigate the crashing sound. She found Ernest in the vestibule, lying in a pool of blood, his gun by his side. She was shocked but not surprised. After phoning Dr. Saviers, she went to the Atkinsons', the friends who owned the local grocery store and had helped with negotiations for the Ketchum house. She took a tranquilizer to stop her shaking, went to bed for a while in the apartment above the store, and then began the tasks she must have long anticipated. She phoned Ernest's sons, a few friends, and their lawyer, Alfred Smith; made arrangements at the Ketchum Cemetery for the funeral; and took and hid Ernest's double-barreled Boss shotgun. Later, she had the gun cut up and buried by the local blacksmith. Posterity would have no grim souvenir of the man who had been her lover, her friend, and to whom she had been a very thoughtful, practical nurse.

Epilogue

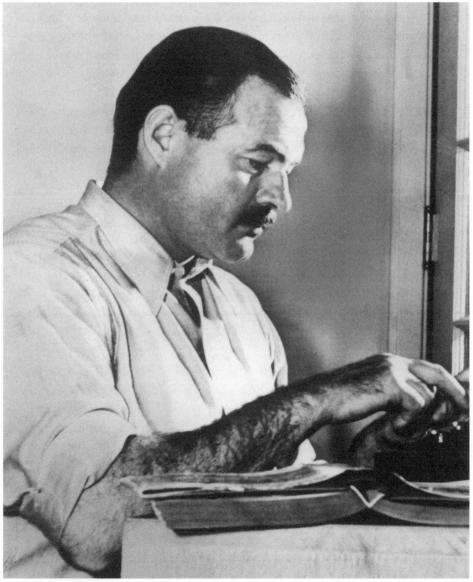

Figure 7.1. Ernest Hemingway circa 1940.
"Once writing has become your major vice and greatest pleasure only death can stop it."[1]
Photofest.

ON JULY 6, 1961, FRIENDS AND FAMILY GATHERED IN KETCHUM, IDAHO, to say goodbye to Ernest. His body was transported from the funeral home in nearby Hailey to the Ketchum Cemetery, where a small group of family members and fifty invited friends were waiting. Under blue skies with the Sawtooth Mountains as a backdrop, Father Robert J. Waldmann, the local priest, conducted a brief Catholic graveside committal service and the legendary writer was interred. Years later, Bumby (John "Jack"), Jack's daughter, Margaux, Gregory, and finally Mary would be placed in nearby graves.

Bill Horne, the honorary pallbearer, brought messages of condolence from Ernest's Section IV ambulance driver friends, who had gathered for a reunion near Chicago the weekend of the suicide. Gianfranco Ivancich, Adriana's brother, came from Venice, and Charlie Thompson traveled from Key West. Bill Horne recalled, "Everybody who was there loved Ernie."[2] Being both competent and gracious, Mary entertained the family at dinner the night before the service, while the Hornes hosted a dinner for Ernest's friends from out of town. Ernest's brother, Leicester, commented, "It seemed to me Ernest would have approved of it all."[3] However, as it had been with Leicester, Ernest's relationship with each of the attendees had, at some point, been confrontational. Yet almost all of them would later pen a book detailing their relationship with the man they had loved and lost.

After the funeral, Alfred Rice, Ernest's lawyer, read the September 1955 will to his sons and Mary in the living room of the Ketchum house. The entirety of Ernest's estate was bequeathed to Mary—all cash, securities, real estate in the United States and abroad, and the copyrights to all Ernest's published and unpublished works. Though Rice proposed the creation of a trust into which royalties from foreign publication of Ernest's books would be divided equally among Mary and his three sons, Mary controlled and managed his estate with shrewdness and tenacity for the next twenty-five years. She reviewed his unpublished manuscripts, then edited and published *A Moveable Feast*, *Islands in the Stream*, and *Garden of Eden*, and approved the publication of *Selected Letters 1917–1961*, edited by Carlos Baker.

Figure 7.2. Ernest's funeral at the cemetery in Ketchum, Idaho, 1961. *Alamy.*

Several days after the funeral, Mary received a phone call from Cuba's minister of foreign affairs who wished to acquire the Finca to be used as a *momumento* to Ernest. Knowing that the Cuban government would confiscate the property, she negotiated with the Castro government to allow her to return to Cuba to remove Ernest's literary properties and personal papers and bring them back to the United States. Then, because US citizens were prohibited to travel to Cuba, Mary called Bill Walton and asked him to negotiate with his friend, President Kennedy, to provide permission for a return trip to Havana as well as exit and reentry permits to the United States.

When Mary arrived at Finca Vigia, she headed to the three-tiered file cabinet in the library and pulled out the envelop marked, "Important to be Opened in Case of My Death" and dated May 24, 1958. She read Ernest's message to his executors: "It is my wish that none of the letters written by me during my lifetime shall be published. Accordingly, I hereby request and direct you not to publish or consent to the publication by others, of any such letters."[4] Then Mary packed up his letters, notes, photographs, and manuscripts and loaded them on to a shrimp boat headed for Miami. Later, she asked Bill Walton to negotiate with Jacqueline Kennedy to create a Hemingway Room in the newly designed John F. Kennedy Presidential Library and Museum in Boston, creating the space that currently houses the vast Ernest Hemingway Collection.

While she was still in Cuba, Gregorio Fuentes, Ernest's loyal crewman, asked about the *Pilar*. Mary considered having him take the boat out in the Gulf Stream and sink her, but in the end the *Pilar* was laid to rest in a cradle on the tennis court of the Finca, and the house and its contents were gifted to the Cuban people. When matters in Cuba were settled, Mary returned to the United States, lived in the Ketchum house for a while, then gave it to the Idaho Nature Conservancy and moved permanently to an apartment on 65th Street in New York City.

Until her death, Mary guarded Ernest's reputation. When Cuba issued a commemorative postage stamp in Ernest's honor in 1964, Mary worried that Ernest might be perceived as "a big Castro man."[5] She asked her friend, Quentin Reynolds, to write to J. Edgar Hoover to tell him that the stamp was not sanctioned by Ernest or anyone in his family. At

Mary's direction, Reynolds's letter emphasized that Ernest did not know Castro well, that he hated Batista, and that he, like millions, welcomed anyone who could oust the dictator. No action was taken by the Federal Bureau of Investigation in relation to the commemorative stamp. However, Reynolds's letter was placed in Ernest's Federal Bureau of Investigation file with a handwritten notation from Hoover saying, "Ernest was a tough guy and always for the underdog."[6]

In 1966, Mary sued A. E. Hotchner for revealing the details leading up to Ernest's suicide in his biography, *Papa Hemingway*. Though anyone who knew Ernest understood he would not have had an accident with a gun, at the time of his death, Mary told reporters it was an accident. Mary lost the case against Hotchner, and five years after Ernest's death she finally admitted that he died of self-inflicted gunshots.

Mary died on November 26, 1986, in St. Luke's Hospital at age seventy-eight after a prolonged illness. As was stipulated in her will, she was buried in Ketchum next to Ernest.

Figure 7.3. Mary Hemingway with Fidel Castro.
Ernest Hemingway Collection. John F. Kennedy Presidential Library and Museum, Boston, Massachusetts.

Given Ernest's zest for living, his vast productivity as a writer, and the high profile created by his adventures and exploits, he won and lost many friends. Long before it was over, his life's story was fertile territory for critics. Throughout his life, he longed for the approval of his parents, and they desperately tried to find some piece of his adult life or his writing of which they could approve. Yet both Ernest and his parents knew the closeness of the boyhood years in Oak Park would never be regained. The chasm in values and lifestyles had become too wide. Though his boyhood love of hunting and fishing provided the interest and skills for a lifetime of adventures, and the Midwestern work ethic and the sound educational background in reading, writing, and the arts provided resources necessary for a successful career as a writer, once out of Oak Park, Ernest discovered cigarettes, alcohol, women, and a vocabulary that would not be tolerated in the place he once called home.

The women who loved and supported him both emotionally and financially also joined the list of critics. Martha probably was the most bitter. From the beginning of their marriage, Martha and Ernest were literary rivals. Though Ernest encouraged Martha to write during the Spanish Civil War, as her career with *Collier's* progressed, he didn't want her to leave his side and go on reporting adventures of her own.

Martha thought living "in sin" was wonderful but agreed to marry Ernest. However, being known simply as Mrs. Hemingway caused Martha unending irritation, especially when critics tried to find parallels between her writing style and that of her more celebrated husband's. She had written two novels before meeting Ernest and continued writing for almost a half-century after leaving him. She didn't want to be "a footnote to somebody else's life."[7]

When Ernest replaced her as a war correspondent for *Collier's*, she independently reported on the D-Day invasion and chose to be permanently separated from him emotionally, physically, and financially. She was the only one of Ernest's wives to leave him, and he never forgave her for it. But she, too, remained bitter even after their divorce, saying "I weep for the eight years I spent . . . worshipping his image with him, and I weep for whatever else I was cheated of due to that time-serving."[8]

After World War II, Martha adopted a son in Italy and raised him, largely on her own, in Mexico and other countries, where she supported herself by writing a string of "bilge" short stories and articles for women's magazines. She received no money from Ernest. Because he had sued her for desertion, under Cuban law, Ernest had the right to everything that belonged to Martha. He kept everything that was hers, including her clothes, the typewriter on which she had written her books, and the funds in her Cuban bank account. When Martha requested her family's monogrammed silver, china, and crystal that her mother had given to her, it was shipped to her at her expense, but arrived at her rented house in Mexico badly damaged.

With limited resources, Martha moved from Cuba to Italy to Mexico to Kenya until finally settling in Britain, where she spent her last fifteen years shuttling between a small cottage in Wales, an apartment in London, and the world's trouble spots. Her South Kensington apartment became a salon for writers and foreign correspondents, and her tenacity for reporting and what it meant to be a truly independent woman remained one of the most fascinating aspects of her writing. She convinced British pilots to let her ride along on night bombing raids over Germany, and when the Allies liberated Dachau, she was there to write about it, saying, "Behind the barbed wire and the electric fence, the skeletons sat in the sun and searched themselves for lice. They have no age and no faces; they all look alike and like nothing you will ever see if you are lucky."[9]

Martha covered the Vietnam War, the Nicaraguan Contra Revolution, the Arab–Israeli conflict, and, at the age of eighty-one, the US invasion of Panama. She retired from journalism in the early 1990s when an unsuccessful operation for cataracts left her nearly blind. Unable to read her own manuscripts and suffering from ovarian cancer, she died in London on February 15, 1998, by swallowing a cyanide capsule. She is remembered today as an intrepid female journalist, and, though she wouldn't like it, as Ernest's third wife, and Bumby's (Jack Hemingway's) "favorite other mother."[10]

Figure 7.4. Martha Gellhorn.
She didn't want to be a footnote to somebody else's life.
Steve Pyke/Getty Images.

Ernest's 1940 divorce from Pauline was the most complicated of his separations. Pauline had supported Ernest emotionally and financially and with great difficulty had borne him two sons. She looked the other way during his flirtation with Jane Mason, but when Ernest wanted to leave her to marry Martha, she was angry and did not make the separation easy for him. Because of Pauline and Uncle Gus's generosity, Ernest had enjoyed a comfortable house, a car, and trips to Spain and Africa that enriched his writing. His family, too, was financially secure as Pauline opened trust funds for Patrick, Gregory, and even Bumby and Ernest's mother, Grace. As separation agreements neared being settled, Pauline countered by demanding more money. Though Pauline did not need financial support, money symbolized to her Ernest's admission that she had been wronged.

However, Ernest thought differently. He believed since Pauline had stolen him from Hadley, she was getting what she deserved. The battle continued. The more Ernest wanted to be with Martha, the more Pauline delayed, and the more Ernest insisted that her devout Catholicism had ruined his sex life. As time passed, Ernest felt he was being manipulated by Pauline and advised Max Perkins to "never marry a rich bitch . . . they (have) a way of sensing your soft spots and upping the price."[11]

When they finally reached a settlement, Pauline received five hundred dollars a month, 60 percent of the Key West house, and the right to lease or rent the house providing she paid the taxes and insurance. Pauline agreed to never keep the boys from their father, and plans were made for the boys to go to Sun Valley to be with Ernest and Martha for the 1940 duck-hunting season. Pauline filed for divorce in Miami then went to San Franisco to be with her sister, Ginny. She rented an apartment on Telegraph Hill that had views of San Francisco Bay and planned to divide her time between Key West and San Francisco.

After the divorce, Pauline continued to live in Key West with frequent visits to California but was troubled by Gregory's gender identity issues. Apparently, when Pauline left Gregory to go on the safari in 1933–1934, the boy missed his mother so much, he would take her stockings from her dresser and touch and smell them. As he matured, he had an affinity for feminine objects and clothing. At the age of twelve, he was caught wearing Martha Gellhorn's stockings, causing an outburst of anger from his father. When he was fourteen, Mary accused the maid of stealing her lingerie but later discovered the items under Gregory's mattress. Though Gregory continued to struggle with his sexual identity, he went on to attend the Canterbury School, a Catholic preparatory school in Connecticut, graduated in 1949, and attended St. John's College in Annapolis but dropped out after a year. When he moved to California in 1951, he was arrested for entering the women's bathroom in a Los Angeles movie

Figure 7.5. Pauline Pfieffer Hemingway and Mary Hemingway.
Ernest Hemingway Collection. John F. Kennedy Presidential Library and Museum, Boston, Massachusetts.

theater dressed in women's clothing. Pauline hired an attorney to deal with the arrest and phoned Ernest. He exploded in anger and, for over an hour, harangued Pauline and blamed her for Gregory's behavior.

Unbeknownst to anyone in the family, Pauline had an adrenal gland tumor. The stress of the argumentative phone call caused her adrenaline to spike, and she died suddenly that night. When Gregory was accepted to medical school in Miami in 1959, he investigated his mother's death. He found that she'd suffered from adrenal cancer, and in studying her autopsy report, he concluded that the phone call with Ernest had caused the tumor to secrete excessive adrenaline and then stop, resulting in a change in blood pressure that caused his mother to go into acute shock and die.

Pauline was fifty-six when she died on October 1, 1951, and was buried in Hollywood Memorial Cemetery. Her family home and barn in Piggott, Arkansas, were placed on the National Register of Historic Places in 1982 and now constitute the Hemingway-Pfeiffer Museum and Educational Center.

Because of *A Moveable Feast*, Hadley is perhaps the most positively remembered of Ernest's wives. Like Pauline, she supported Ernest both emotionally and financially, but after Ernest left her to marry Pauline, she went on to have a happy and productive life. Though Ernest later said he wished he had died before he loved anyone but her, Hadley had the opportunity to love another.

Hadley became aware of Ernest's affair with Pauline in the spring of 1926. She endured Pauline's presence in Pamplona that July and, on their return to Paris, gave Ernest the hundred-day ultimatum: She said if he and Pauline still wanted to be together after the separation, then she would consent to a divorce. In less than one hundred days, however, Hadley recognized her marriage to Ernest was over and moved with Bumby to an apartment at 35 rue des Fleurus near Gertrude Stein and Alice B. Toklas's salon. She made a list of personal articles and furniture she wanted for the new flat, and Ernest rented a wheelbarrow to move them from the Notre Dame des Champs flat to rue du Fleurus. Ernest made several trips hauling furniture, family silver, and china, and Hadley pretended to be unmoved each time he burst into tears over some sentimental item.

Ernest was an emotional mess, but Hadley stoically clarified her decision to divorce, later writing, "the entire problem belongs to you two—I am not responsible for your future welfare. . . . I took you originally for better, for worse (and meant it!) but in the case of you marrying some one else, I can stand by my vow only as an outside friend."[12] Ernest appreciated Hadley's brave acceptance of the situation and instructed Scribner's to assign to her all the royalties from *The Sun Also Rises*. Hadley replied, "The gift from you to me of your royalties on *The Sun Also Rises* is very acceptable and I can't see a reason just now why I should refuse it. Thank you a lot."[13]

Hadley encouraged Ernest to see Bumby as much as he wished and made the divorce easy for their son. She told him Ernest and Pauline were very much in love and never let him know that something out of the ordinary had happened. Bumby's adult memories of living alone with his mother in Paris were positive and loving. He later said, "I came to love the sound of the rain on the slate mansard roof, and the reassurance of sleeping so near to her and going from the little alcove to her big warm bed in the early morning."[14]

Ernest and Hadley divorced in April 1927, and Ernest married Pauline in May the same year. But not long after her divorce was finalized, Hadley met Paul Mowrer, a foreign correspondent for the *Chicago Daily News*. He covered the front during the First Balkan War and the Great War in Europe from 1914 to 1918. In 1921, he was the special correspondent for the Disarmament Conference, and in 1929 he was awarded the first Pulitzer Prize for Correspondence while at the *Chicago Daily News*.

Paul was married when they met, but despite their immediate attraction, their courtship lasted five years. On July 3, 1933, Hadley and Paul were married in London and soon moved back to the United States to Lake Bluff, Illinois, a suburb of Chicago. As time passed, Paul developed a warm relationship with Bumby, and Hadley continued to receive royalties from *The Sun Also Rises* book as well as the 1957 film.

Hadley only saw Ernest twice after their divorce. In July 1939, she and Paul ran into him while vacationing in Wyoming, and then saw him

Figure 7.6. Hadley Richardson Hemingway Mowrer.
"I can stand by my vow only as an outside friend."
Ernest Hemingway Collection. John F. Kennedy Presidential Library and Museum, Boston, Massachusetts.

again at a brief and spontaneous meeting in Paris. Though at the time of their divorce, Hadley burned the letters Ernest had written during their courtship, Ernest's later letters to her survived. He wrote to "Dearest Hadley" throughout his lifetime. His letters focused on his love, concern, and support for Bumby, but also were filled with affection for her. As time progressed, his appreciation of the love and the emotional and financial support she provided during the six years they were married grew. Even after she married Paul, Ernest continued to end his letters with warm sentiments, saying "Much love to you and all my best to Paul. I admire you both very much."[15]

Hadley died on January 22, 1979, in Lakeland, Florida, at the age of eighty-seven and is buried in Tamworth, New Hampshire, at Chocorua Cemetery. Her life with Ernest during the Paris years is immortalized not only in *A Moveable Feast*, but also in the fictional account of their time together in Paula McLain's *The Paris Wife*.

Letters balanced Ernest's needs for serious writing with his needs for friendship and reflection. He wrote and received many letters, but probably the most hurtful and influential letter he ever received was the 1919 Dear John letter from Agnes von Kurowsky.

Ernest and Agnes met in Milan at the Red Cross at the Army Hospital during World War I. Though she was seven years his senior and he was only nineteen, Ernest fell in love with her and believed they would marry. However, after he returned to Oak Park in March of 1919, Agnes rejected Ernest, informing him in a letter that she was planning to marry someone else, an Italian officer she had met in Florence. Though Agnes never, in fact, married the Italian officer, later disclosed as Domenico Caracciolo, Ernest was heartbroken. The rejection, however, motivated him to use the wrenching experience to create one of his bestselling novels, *A Farewell to Arms*. Agnes's identity as the basis for the character Catherine Barkley was not widely known until Ernest's brother, Leicester, published *My Brother: Ernest Hemingway* in 1961. Agnes had never revealed she was the model for Catherine Barkley because she did not relish the transformation of her role as his nurse into his consenting sexual partner.

After the war, Agnes spent time in New York, then was sent by the American Red Cross to Romania for two years. After another two years in New York, she went to Haiti and served as director of nurses for country's public health service. While stationed there, she married Howard Preston ("Pete") Garner in 1928 but obtained a quick divorce after her Haitian assignment was completed. She married a second time to William Stanfield, a widower with three children, in 1934. She remained married to Stanfield until her death in Gulfport, Florida, on November 25, 1984, at the age of ninety-two.

Though Dominico Caracciolo, the Italian officer she never married, made her burn her letters from Ernest, she kept photographs of herself and Ernest during their time together in Italy. Having been trained as a librarian as well as a nurse, Agnes Stanfield worked in the Key West Library while she lived in Florida. Thinking Ernest might be interested in the photos, Agnes offered the photos to another librarian, Betty Bruce, who was Ernest's friend. When Betty contacted Ernest about the photos, he told her to send them to Scribner's. After Betty reluctantly shared Ernest's reaction and personal rejection of the photographs, Agnes just laughed and explained Ernest probably was still angry for being turned down by her when he was nineteen. The photographs now reside in The Hemingway Collection at the John F. Kennedy Presidential Library and Museum, while the Dear John letter is the crown jewel of the Ernest Hemingway Foundation archives in Oak Park.

While Agnes von Kurowsky denied being the model for Catherine Barkley until her final years, when *Across the River and Into the Trees* was eventually released in Italy, Adriana Ivancich declared she was Renata in an article she wrote for *Epoca* magazine and in her memoir, *La Torre Bianca* (*The White Tower*). Though *Across the River and Into the Trees* was an embarrassment to Adriana's aristocratic family, the impact of the novel on Adriana's life is not totally clear. She married twice, bore two sons, but suffered from depression and hanged herself from a tree in 1983. Before her death, however, she confessed she was the model for Renata and sold her letters from Ernest via auction at Christie's for seventeen thousand dollars in 1969. Though any secret details of her relationship with Ernest

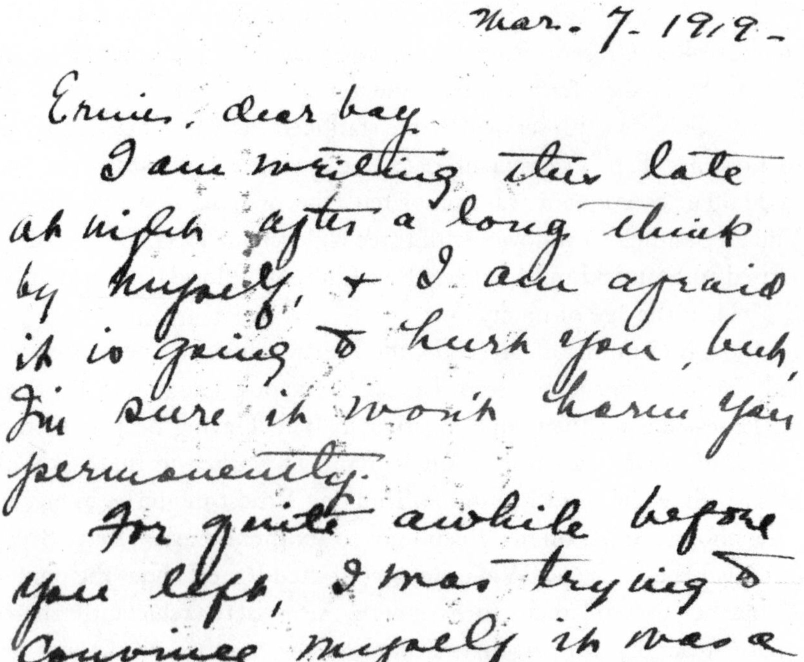

Mar. 7. 1919 -

Ernie, dear boy,

I am writing this late
at night, after a long think
by myself, + I am afraid
it is going to hurt you, but,
I'm sure it won't harm you
permanently.

For quite awhile before
you left, I was trying to
convince myself it was a
real love-affair, because,
we always seemed to dis-
agree. + the arguments always
wore me out so that I finally
gave in to keep you from
doing something desparate...
Now, after a couple of months
away from you, I know

Figure 7.7. Ernie, Dear Boy letter.
*Waring Jones Collection. Ernest Hemingway Foundation of Oak Park Archives,
Oak Park Public Library Special Collections, Oak Park, Illinois.*

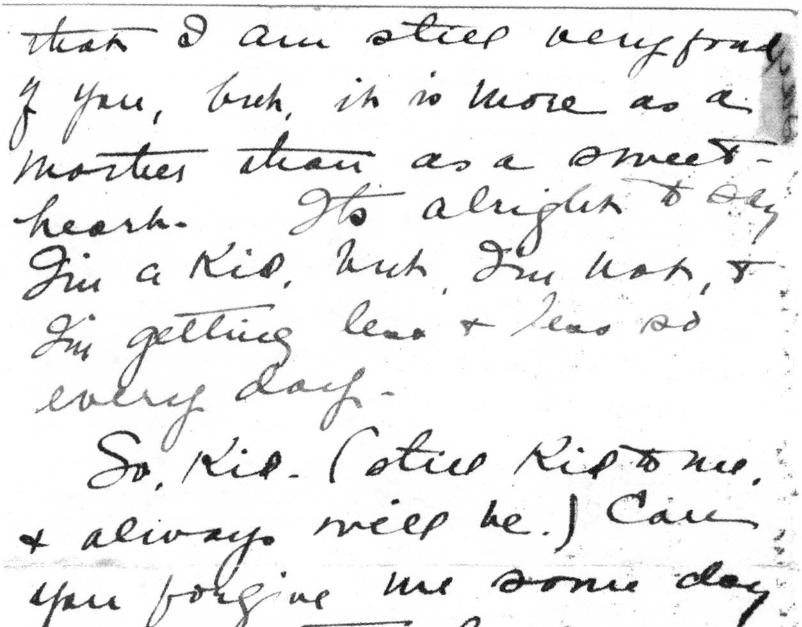

that I am still very fond
of you, but, it is more as a
mother than as a sweet-
heart. It's alright to say
I'm a Kid, but, I'm not, +
I'm getting less + less so
every day.

So, Kid. (still Kid to me,
+ always will be.) Can
you forgive me some day
for unwillingly deceiving
you? You know I'm not
really bad, + don't mean to
do wrong, + now, I realize
it was my fault in the
beginning that you cared
for me, + regret it from the
bottom of my heart.

Figure 7.7. Ernie, Dear Boy letter (continued)

But, I am now & always will be too old, & that's the truth, & I can't get away from the fact that you're just a boy — a kid.

I somehow feel that some day I'll have reason to be proud of you, but, dear boy, I can't wait for that day, & it is wrong to hurry a career.

I tried hard to make you understand a bit of what I was thinking on the trip from Padua to Milan, but you acted like a spoiled child, & I couldn't keep on hurting you. Now I only have the courage because I'm far away.

Then — & believe me when I say this is sudden for me, too — I expect to be married soon. And I hope & pray that after you have thought things out, you'll be able to forgive me & start a wonderful career, & show what a man you really are.

Ever admiringly & fondly
Your friend —
Aggie

Figure 7.7. Ernie, Dear Boy letter (continued)

contained in her memoir are somewhat guarded as copyright laws, and Ernest's will has prohibited the book from being released in the United States, some sixty-nine of their letters now reside in The Hemingway Collection at the John F. Kennedy Presidential Library and Museum and at the University of Texas.

Ernest, along with his wives, his lovers, his children, and his friends were voluminous letter writers. They never intended for their correspondence to be published, but their letters tell their stories and track their emotions. Ernest's letters also reveal his internal conflicts. He enjoyed the expensive pastimes of the wealthy but was critical of their moral code and thought wealth destroyed writers. He loved each of his wives but inevitably needed to escape married life with a new woman in a new frontier. Given his Victorian upbringing, he was compelled to marry each of the women he loved, but a monogamous marriage was challenged by his need to move on. As in other letters, Ernest's conflicts are revealed in his 1925 letter to F. Scott Fitzgerld. Ernest explained that his idea of heaven would include "two houses: one where I would have my wife and children and be monogamous and love them truly and well and the other where I would have my nine beautiful mistresses on nine different floors."[16]

While married to Pauline, Ernest attempted to fulfill his idea of heaven. Pauline provided a stable, well-functioning home life while Ernest simultaneously enjoyed the beauty and daring of Jane Mason. He drew energy from his adulterous relationship with Jane and wrote numerous articles for *Esquire*. His articles contributed to his image as a legendary sportsman and made a valuable contribution to the magazine's success and the eventual wealth of the magazine's founder and publisher, Arnold Gingrich. Ironically, Jane Mason eventually moved on to marry Gingrich, who, thanks in part to Ernest, became wealthy enough to support her expensive adventures and exotic habits.

Jane had a stroke at age fifty-five and was a semi-invalid for the rest of her life, but she is immortalized in Ernest's characterizations of Margot Macomber and Helene Bradley. Though the characters Margot Macomber and Helene Bradley do not shed favorable light on Ernest's "rich bitch" memories of Jane, Jane accepted the characterizations and never forgot Ernest. At her death in 1981, her bedside table contained the photos of both Ernest Hemingway and Arnold Gingrich.

Ernest indulged his conflicts and his need to seek experiences that inspired content for his writing. By the end of his life, the boy from Oak Park forged a new set of values and a code for living in the post–World War I world and developed a style of writing that was embraced and translated around the world. In addition to garnering every prize available to a writer, he married women who adored him, fathered handsome children, owned multiple houses in exotic settings, accumulated a valuable art collection, and engaged in daring adventures that captivated a worldwide audience. He more than fulfilled his high school classmates' prophecy that "None are to be found more clever than Ernie."[17]

The boy from Oak Park became a citizen of the world. Before he was forty, he had called Italy, France, Switzerland, Spain, Canada, Key West, and Cuba home. His friends around the world included Russian journalists, Spanish bullfighters, Cuban fishermen, US presidents, and glamorous movie stars. Because his novels and short stories were made into movies, he considered Ava Gardner, Rita Hayworth, Ingrid Berman, and Gary Cooper as some of his closest friends.

Though comfortable on a small fishing boat or on the frontline of a battlefield, he also moved with ease into the world of the rich and famous. Traveling back to the States aboard the *Ile de France* in 1934, he met Marlene Dietrich in the ship's dining room. She resisted being seated because she did not want to be the thirteenth person at the table. Ernest reacted quickly by offering to be the fourteenth man at the table and began a long friendship with the star. He affectionately called her "The Kraut." Later, she documented her own feelings in a *New York Herald Tribune* article, calling Ernest "the most fascinating man I know."[18]

Characteristic of many of his friendships, Ernest played the role of Marlene's teacher or mentor. She saw him as a "huge rock" and believed "if more people had friends like Ernest there would be fewer analysts."[19] Once when she was torn with indecision about a lucrative job offer, he counseled her not to do what she sincerely didn't want to do, saying "Never confuse movement with action."[20] Those five words provided the actress with a philosophy of life just as the words and actions of the

Figure 7.8. Marlene Dietrich with the most fascinating man she knew. *PictureLux/The Hollywood Archive/Alamy.*

code heroes in Ernest's novels and short stories provided his readers with a set of rules for living in the post–World War I world.

Though Ernest was the teacher, Marlene was a keen student. She understood his rules for living, appreciated the various ways in he put them into action, and understood that he "found time to do the things most men only dream about."[21] Talking about the most fascinating man she knew, she said he was "the most positive life force I have ever encountered."[22] Their friendship survived twenty-seven years—from the time they met until Ernest's death. It was nourished by long distance phone calls, letters, transatlantic crossings aboard the same ships, dinners at 21 Club in New York, and meetings at the Ritz Hotel in Paris.

Ernest was happiest when he was writing. When he finished *Across the River and Into the Trees*, he filled his sense of emptiness and boredom by writing to Marlene:

My dearest Marlene:
    I write this early in the morning, the hour that poor people and the soldiers and sailors wake from habit, to send you small letter for if you are lonely or anything. Yesterday I died with my Colonel for the last time and said good-bye to the girl and it was worse than any other time. But the last page proofs are done now. I did them in one day a night and then yesterday.
    Now I must not try to think about it and the hell with everything.
    I always tell you everything so I tell you that saying goodbye to that girl in real life was not my true vocation. Now I don't know if I will ever see her again. But if I do and I have to say good-bye to her, and I will, it will not be fun either. I hope you do not mind me being an unfaithful because basically I am a faithful. One time I had a wonderful plan and resolve to only love one person. This plan was known as the Seven Year Monogamy Plan. It went to hell too.
    So now I have no plan. I should have some money and I suppose that should make me happy. Then there is this war that I am not interested in. We go now on the *Pilar* on the ocean for three days and I will try to fish intelligently and shoot beer cans with a pistol with my best ability, rapidity and finesse.

I was thinking about you last night when I couldn't sleep and I thought how worse women's problems are than mens. Men have a few too. I guess the true extent of one's problems (Dr. Hemingstein the Philosopher) is measured by the capacity of your heart to love anything when there is no good end to it.

I've been in love (truly) with five women, the Spanish Republic and the 4th Infantry Division. The women's end like womens and, I guess. I knew we were beaten in Spain when we lost Irun in 36 and I stuck around for two and a half years with my heart and two balls and less than 1000 pieces of artillery for a 650 mile front. You could ask your old man what that means. The mortars all home made.

I loved Miss Martha I guess but I couldn't stand her and she lied to me for eight years that she absolutely couldn't have a baby. Well we'll leave women out of this except I fall in love with you bad and you're always in love with some jerk. I get a wonderful girl like Mary and they hit my heart again like with an 88. During this time I love the 4th Inf. Div. and 2,569 casualties out of a strength of 12,500 to 13,000. I love my Black Dog and he loves me and he is getting old. I loved a lovely grey Persian named Princessa and she died last week of old age.

This letter is a lot of shit or should we polite and talk German and say cabbage. I still love practically god-damn everything and I certainly love you my damn, bloody hero. But Christ I'm tired and I get bored shit-less when I finish something. Think you will like book. Have really worked on it. If you like it one half as much as I like you in *A Foreign Affair* I'll be happy.

Will have Scribner's send you the first one they print.

You can read it while you fly over the Koreans. Make slow rolls and entertain them.

I love you very much,
Papa[23]

Ernest told Marlene everything. He knew she understood him because she was the daring female version of himself. Though he loved her, he felt free to talk candidly about his other loves. Adriana, Martha, Hadley, and Mary are all referenced in his letter to Marlene. Given their relationship, she most likely understood the complexities surrounding his desire to be faithful. She also couldn't help but know that he had a reputation for being a bully, for being egotistical, and for being unfaithful. But, like others, she found him to be "most fascinating" because he did "the things most men only dream about."[24]

ACKNOWLEDGMENTS

Much has been written about the extraordinary life of Ernest Hemingway. The works of James Mellow, Bernice Kert, and Valerie Hemingway have been extremely helpful in filling in the details of Hemingway's adventures as well as the places he lived, the women he loved, and experiences that influenced his novels, short stories, and non-fiction articles.

Yet the major contribution to understanding Hemingway's passions came from reading the letters he wrote and the letters he received. It was his correspondence that revealed his ambition, his anger, and his heartbreak, as well as his extraordinary sense of humor. I am grateful to Sandra Spanier and the many contributors to The Hemingway Letters Project. Though Ernest never intended for his letters to be published, the wealth of information contained in the first six volumes of the letters project is a gift to anyone interested in the life and work of Ernest Hemingway.

Photographs also helped to tell Ernest's story. Ernest's father, Dr. Clarence Hemingway, was an avid photographer, and long before the world became acquainted with the life of Ernest Hemingway, Clarence was taking photographs of his handsome and adventurous son. Thanks to the photograph collections of Marcelline Hemingway Stanford and Waring Jones, Ernest's early life has been preserved, and I am grateful to Kathleen Spale and Carrie Vacon, archivists at the Oak Park Public Library, and the Ernest Hemingway Foundation of Oak Park for providing images from these valuable collections.

I also wish to acknowledge the vision of Mary Hemingway, Ernest's widow, and Jacqueline Kennedy, President Kennedy's widow, that led to the creation of a sizable space at the John F. Kennedy Presidential Library and Museum in Boston for gathering and preserving Ernest's letters, manuscripts, Grace Hall Hemingway's Memory Books, and over ten thousand photographs. I am grateful to Maryrose Grossman, audio-visual reference archivist of the Hemingway Collection, for her extraordinary help in identifying, scanning, and providing photos relevant to Hemingway's passions from the vast Hemingway Collection housed at the library in Boston.

Finally, throughout his life, Ernest followed his family's tradition of living in two places at the same time. As a child it was Oak Park and Walloon Lake. At the end of his life, it was San Francisco de Paula, Cuba, and Ketchum, Idaho, but when he wasn't at one of his homes, he was reporting on a war in Europe or hunting for big game in Africa or fishing in the Gulf of Mexico. This lifestyle led to experiences that contributed to his legend as well as his writing, but it made writing about him difficult. I am grateful to acquisitions editors Brittany Stoner and Justine Connelly for their help in organizing a logical narrative of Hemingway's life. Their thoughtful questions and careful editing were meaningful in making *Hemingway's Passions* understandable and hopefully interesting to the reader.

CHRONOLOGY

November 9, 1891	Elizabeth Hadley Richardson is born to James and Florence Wyman Richardson in St. Louis, Missouri.
January 5, 1892	Agnes von Kurowsky is born to Paul and Agnes von Kurowsky in Philadelphia, Pennsylvania.
July 22, 1895	Pauline Pfeiffer is born to Paul and Mary Alice Peiffer in Parkersburg, Iowa.
July 21, 1899	Ernest Miller Hemingway is born to Dr. Clarence Hemingway and Grace Hall Hemingway in Oak Park, Illinois.
April 5, 1908	Mary Welsh is born to Thomas and Adeline Beehler Welsh in Walker, Minnesota.
November 8, 1908	Martha Gellhorn is born to Dr. George and Edna Fischel Gellhorn in St. Louis, Missouri.
June 1917	Ernest graduates from Oak Park High School.
October 1917	Ernest moves to Kansas City and works as a cub reporter for the *Kansas City Star*.
May 1918	Ernest goes to Italy as a Red Cross ambulance driver during World War I.
July 8, 1918	Ernest is injured by an Austrian mortar shell near Fossalta di Piave, Italy.
July 11, 1918	Agnes von Kurowsky arrives at the American Red Cross Hospital in Milan.
July 17, 1918	Ernest arrives at the American Red Cross Hospital in Milan.

January 1, 1919	Ernest returns to Oak Park.
March 7, 1919	Ernest receives the Dear John letter from Agnes von Kurowsky.
January–May 1920	Ernest lives in Toronto with the Connable family and writes occasional articles for the *Toronto Star*.
October 1920	Ernest meets Hadley Richardson at the home of Kenley and Doodles Smith in Chicago.
December 1920	Ernest begins writing for the *Cooperative Commonwealth* in Chicago.
September 3, 1921	Ernest marries Hadley Richardson in Horton Bay, Michigan, and then moves with Hadley to 1239 N. Dearborn Street in Chicago.
December 8, 1921	Ernest and Hadley sail for France aboard the *Leopoldina* and move to 74 rue du Cardinal Lemoine, Paris. Ernest works as a freelance writer for the *Toronto Star*.
July 1923	Ernest takes his first trip to Spain with Robert McAlmond and Bill Bird.
August 1923	*Three Stories and Ten Poems* is published by Robert McAlmond's Contact Editions in Paris.
October 1923	Ernest and Hadley move to 1599 Bathurst Street in Toronto, where Ernest works as a reporter for the *Toronto Star*.
October 10, 1923	John Hadley Nicanor Hemingway (Bumby) is born in Toronto.
January 1924	Ernest, Hadley, and Bumby return to Paris, where Ernest edits the *Transatlantic Review*. The family lives above the sawmill at 113 rue Notre Dame des Champs.
April 1924	*in our time* is published by the Three Mountains Press.
July 1924	Ernest and Hadley take their first trip to Pamplona, Spain, for the Festival of San Fermin.

June–July 1925	Ernest and Hadley, joined by Pauline Pfeiffer, take their second trip to Pamplona, Spain, for the Festival of San Fermin.
October 1925	*in our time* is published by Boni & Liveright.
May 1926	*Torrents of Spring* is published by Scribner's.
June–July 1926	Ernest and Hadley, joined by Pauline Pfeiffer, take their third trip to Pamplona, Spain, for the Festival of San Fermin.
October 1926	*The Sun Also Rises* is published by Scribner's.
April 14, 1927	Hadley divorces Ernest.
May 10, 1927	Ernest marries Pauline Pfeiffer in Paris.
October 1927	*Men Without Women* is published by Scribner's.
March 1928	Ernest and Pauline leave Paris and move to an apartment in Key West, Florida.
June 28, 1928	Patrick Hemingway is born in Kansas City.
December 6, 1928	Clarence Hemingway dies of a self-inflected gunshot wound in Oak Park, Illinois.
September 1929	*A Farewell to Arms* is published by Scribner's.
November 11, 1931	Gregory Hemingway is born in Kansas City.
December 1931	Ernest and Pauline and family move to 907 Whitehead Street, Key West, Florida.
September 1932	*Death in the Afternoon* is published by Scribner's.
August 1933	Ernest and Pauline go on an African safari.
May 1934	Ernest orders the *Pilar* from the Wheeler Shipyard in Brooklyn, New York.
October 1935	*Green Hills of Africa* is published by Scribner's.
November 1936	Ernest is hired by the North American Newspaper Alliance as a war correspondent to cover the Spanish Civil War.
December 1936	Ernest meets Martha Gellhorn at Sloppy Joe's Bar in Key West, Florida.

October 1937	*To Have and Have Not* is published by Scribner's.
April 1939	Ernest moves to Finca Vigia near Havana with Martha Gellhorn.
October 21, 1940	*For Whom the Bell Tolls* is published by Scribner's.
November 4, 1940	Pauline divorces Ernest.
November 21, 1940	Ernest marries Martha Gellhorn in Cheyenne, Wyoming.
January 31– May 1941	Ernest and Martha travel to China for a "working honeymoon" and cover the Sino-Japanese War. After spending time in Hawaii, Hong Kong, Namyung, the Canton Front, and Chungking, they return to the United States and then to Cuba.
December 7, 1941	The Japanese attack Pearl Harbor.
May 1942	Ernest initiates Crook Factory counterintelligence activities.
October 8, 1942	Initial entry into Ernest's Federal Bureau of Investigation file by R. Gordon Leddy.
July 1942–July 1943	German submarines are discovered in the Gulf of Mexico; Ernest begins armed patrols aboard the *Pilar*.
May 1944	Ernest is hired by *Collier's* as a war correspondent to cover World War II and flies to London, where he meets Mary Welsh. Martha is released as a war correspondent for *Collier's*.
June 6, 1944	Ernest covers the D-Day invasion for *Collier's* from the vantage point of a landing craft.
June 6, 1944	Martha covers the D-Day invasion as an independent journalist from the vantage point of Omaha Beach.

August 1944	Ernest joins Col. David Bruce in Rambouillet, France, and participates in the liberation of Paris.
August–December 1944	Ernest joins the 22nd Regiment with Col. Buck Lanham and covers the Battle of Hurtgen Forest; meets with Mary Welsh in Paris whenever possible.
March 6, 1945	Ernest departs Paris and returns to Cuba.
May 8, 1945	Mary arrives in Cuba.
December 21, 1945	Ernest divorces Martha.
March 13, 1946	Ernest marries Mary Welsh in Havana.
August 19, 1946	Mary's fallopian tube ruptures, and she loses her baby.
June 13, 1947	Ernest is awarded the Bronze Star at the US Embassy in Havana for "meritorious service as a war correspondent" in France and Germany.
October 1948	Ernest and Mary Hemingway travel to Italy, where Ernest meets Adriana Ivancich.
May 27, 1949	Ernest and Mary return to Cuba.
September 1950	*Across the River and Into the Trees* is published by Scribner's. Adriana and her mother and brother arrive in Cuba.
June 28, 1951	Grace Hall Hemingway dies in Memphis, Tennessee.
October 1, 1951	Pauline Pfeiffer Hemingway dies in Hollywood, California.
September 1952	*The Old Man and the Sea* is published by Scribner's.
May 1953	Ernest is awarded the Pulitzer Prize for *The Old Man and the Sea.*
June 1953–March 1954	Ernest and Mary travel to Spain and Africa. In Africa, they survived two plane crashes.

July 1954	Ernest is awarded the Order of Carlos Manuel de Cepedes, Cuba's highest civilian honor.
October 28, 1954	Ernest is awarded the Nobel Prize for Literature.
December 1957	In Cuba, Ernest begins work on *A Moveable Feast*, published posthumously in 1964.
January 1959	Fidel Castro takes over the governing of Cuba. Batista flees the country.
April 1959	Ernest and Mary purchase a house in Ketchum, Idaho.
	Ernest and Mary travel to Spain. Ernest begins work on *The Dangerous Summer*.
July 21, 1959	Ernest's sixtieth birthday party La Consula.
May 1960	After extensive editing, *The Dangerous Summer* is published in *Life*.
November 1960	Ernest begins treatments for depression at the Mayo Clinic in Rochester, Minnesota.
April 15, 1961	Bay of Pigs invasion in Cuba.
July 2, 1961	Ernest dies of a self-inflected gunshot wound in Ketchum, Idaho.
January 22, 1979	Hadley Richardson Hemingway Mowrer dies in Lakeland, Florida, and is buried at Chocorua Cemetery in Tamworth, New Hampshire.
March 24, 1983	Adriana Ivanich dies in Orbetello, Italy
November 25, 1984	Agnes von Kurowsky dies in Gulfport, Florida
June 1985	The book *Dangerous Summer* is published posthumously by Scribner's.
November 26, 1986	Mary Welsh Hemingway dies in New York, New York, and is buried near Ernest in the Ketchum, Idaho, cemetery.
February 15, 1998	Martha Gellhorn dies in London.

NOTES

DEDICATION

1. Ernest Hemingway to Bill Horne, July 17, 1923, in *Ernest Hemingway: Selected Letters 1917–1961*, 288. Reprinted with the permission of Scribner Publishing Group from *Ernest Hemingway: Selected Letters 1917–1961*, edited by Carlos Baker. Copyright 1981 by Carlos Baker and the Ernest Hemingway Foundation, Inc. All rights reserved.

AUTHOR'S NOTE

1. Ernest Hemingway to Arthur Mizener, May 12, 1950, *Ernest Hemingway: Selected Letters 1917–1961*, edited by Carlos Baker (New York: Scribner's), 695.

PROLOGUE

1. Honoria Murphy Donnelly and Richard N. Billings, *Sara & Gerald: Villa America and After* (New York: Times Books, 1982), 22.

2. Ernest Hemingway, quoted by Grace Hall Hemingway, *Memory Book I*, Hemingway Collection, John F. Kennedy Library, Boston, Massachusetts.

3. Leicester Hemingway, *My Brother, Ernest Hemingway* (Cleveland: World Publishing Company, 1961), 21.

4. Ernest Hemingway, "Indian Camp," *The Complete Short Stories of Ernest Hemingway* (New York: Charles Scribner's Sons, 1987), 70. Copyright © Hemingway Foreign Rights Trust. Reprinted with the permission of Scribner, a division of Simon & Schuster LLC. All rights

reserved. Reprinted by permission of Simon & Schuster (US) and The Random House Group Limited (UK).

5. Ibid.

6. Ernest Hemingway, "Fathers and Sons," *The Complete Short Stories of Ernest Hemingway* (New York: Charles Scribner's Sons, 1987), 374. Copyright © Hemingway Foreign Rights Trust. Reprinted with the permission of Scribner, a division of Simon & Schuster LLC. All rights reserved. Reprinted by permission of Simon & Schuster (US) and The Random House Group Limited (UK).

7. Ibid., 370.

8. Clarence Hemingway, quoted in Marcelline Hemingway Sanford, *At the Hemingways* (Moscoa, ID: University of Idaho Press, 1998), 79.

9. Ibid., 75.

10. Grace Hall Hemingway, *Memory Book II*, Hemingway Collection, John F. Kennedy Library, Boston, Masachusetts.

11. Leicester Hemingway, *My Brother, Ernest Hemingway*, 27.

12. Ernest Hemingway, "Now I Lay Me," *The Complete Short Stories of Ernest Hemingway* (New York: Charles Scribner's Sons, 1987), 277–78. Copyright © Hemingway Foreign Rights Trust. Reprinted with the permission of Scribner, a division of Simon & Schuster LLC. All rights reserved. Reprinted by permission of Simon & Schuster (US) and The Random House Group Limited (UK).

13. Anson Hemingway, Civil War Journal, May 1863, Special Collections Oak Park Public Library, Oak Park, Illinois.

14. Ernest Hemingway, "A Silent, Ghastly Procession," *Dateline: Toronto*, October 20, 1922 (New York: Scribner's, 1985), 232.

15. Fannie Biggs, quoted in Peter Griffin, *Along with Youth* (New York: Oxford University Press, 1985), 25.

16. Ernest Hemingway, "A Ring Lardner on the Bloomington Game," *Trapeze*, 1916.

17. Pete Wellington, quoted in Carlos Baker, *Ernest Hemingway: A Life Story* (New York: Scribner's, 1969), 34.

18. Ernest Hemingway, quoted in Sheridan Baker, *Ernest Hemingway: An Introduction and Interpretation* (Ann Arbor, MI: University of Michigan, 1967), 10.

19. Ernest Hemingway, quoted in Sanford, *At the Hemingways*, 156–57.

20. Ernest Hemingway, quoted in Fannie Biggs, *Memories of Ernest Hemingway*, Yale Collection of American Literature, Beinecke Rare Book and Manuscript Library, Yale University (n.d.).

21. Milford Baker, Milford Baker Diary, June 7, 1918, Carlos Baker papers.

22. Ernest Hemingway, *Death in the Afternoon* (New York: Charles Scribner's Sons, 1932), 135–6. Copyright © Hemingway Foreign Rights Trust. Reprinted with the permission of Scribner, a division of Simon & Schuster LLC. All rights reserved. Reprinted by permission of Simon & Schuster (US) and The Random House Group Limited (UK).

23. Bill Horne, quoted in Virginia Moseley, "Hemingway Remembered," *Barrington Courier-Review*, September 27, 1979, 28–33.

24. Robert Lewis, "Hemingway in Italy," *Journal of Modern Literature* (May 1982): 215.

25. Clarence Hemingway, Letter to Ernest Hemingway, July 17, 1918, Hemingway Collection John F. Kennedy Library, Boston, Massachusetts.

26. Joseph Wood Krutch, "The Nation," quoted in James R. Mellow, *Hemingway: A Life Without Consequences* (New York: Addison Wesley, 1992), 355.

27. Grace Hall Hemingway to Ernest Hemingway, quoted in Kenneth Lynn, *Hemingway*, 357.

28. Ernest Hemingway, Letter to Clarence Hemingway, March 20, 1925, Reprinted with the permission of Scribner, a division of Simon & Schuster LLC, from *Ernest Hemingway: Selected Letters 1917–1961*, edited by Carlos Baker, 153. Copyright © 1981 by Carlos Baker and The Ernest Hemingway Foundation, Inc. All rights reserved.

29. Audre Hannaman, quoted in Mellow, *Hemingway*, 334–35.

30. Ernest Hemingway, quoted in Sanford, *At the Hemingways*, 184.

31. Ernest Hemingway, quoted in "George Plimpton: Interview with Ernest Hemingway," in Baker (ed.), *Hemingway and His Critics*, 34.

AGNES

1. Agnes von Kurowsky, quoted in James R. Mellow, *Hemingway: A Life Without Consequences* (New York: Addison-Wesley Publishing, 1997), 66.

2. Ernest Hemingway, Letter to family, July 21, 1918, Reprinted with the permission of Scribner, a division of Simon & Schuster LLC, from *The Letters of Ernest Hemingway: Volume 1 (1907–1922)*, edited by Sandra Spanier and Robert Trogdon Copyright © (New York: Cambridge University Press, 2011), 117. All rights reserved.

3. Ernest Hemingway, Letter to Grace Hall Hemingway, July 29, 1918, Reprinted with the permission of Scribner, a division of Simon & Schuster LLC, from *The Letters of Ernest Hemingway: Volume 1 (1907–1922)*, edited by Sandra Spanier and Robert Trogdon Copyright © (New York: Cambridge University Press, 2011), 120–21. All rights reserved.

4. Ernest Hemingway, Letter to family, August 4, 1918, Reprinted with the permission of Scribner, a division of Simon & Schuster LLC, from *The Letters of Ernest Hemingway: Volume 1 (1907–1922)*, edited by Sandra Spanier and Robert Trogdon Copyright © (New York: Cambridge University Press, 2011), 123–24. All rights reserved.

5. Ibid.

6. Agnes von Kurowsky, Diary, August 25, 1918, quoted in Mellow, *A Life Without Consequences*, 72.

7. Henry Villard and James Nagel, *Hemingway in Love and War: The Lost Diary of Agnes Von Kurkowsky* (Boston: Northeastern University Press, 1989), 73.

8. Marcelline Hemingway Sanford, Letter to Ernest Hemingway, October 2, 1918, footnote, Reprinted with the permission of Scribner, a division of Simon & Schuster LLC, from *The Letters of Ernest Hemingway: Volume 1 (1907–1922)*, edited by Sandra Spanier and Robert Trogdon Copyright © (New York: Cambridge University Press, 2011), 153–54.

9. Ibid.

10. Ibid.

11. Ibid.

12. Ernest Hemingway, Letter to Marcelline Hemingway, November 23, 1918, Reprinted with the permission of Scribner, a division of Simon & Schuster LLC, from *The Letters of Ernest Hemingway: Volume 1 (1907–1922)*, edited by Sandra Spanier and Robert Trogdon Copyright © (New York: Cambridge University Press, 2011), 156–57. All rights reserved.

13. Agnes von Kurowsky to Ernest Hemingway, October 21, 1918, Hemingway Collection, John F. Kennedy Library, Boston, Massachusetts.

14. Agnes von Kurowsky to Ernest Hemingway, October 25, 1918, Hemingway Collection, John F. Kennedy Library, Boston, Massachusetts.

15. Ernest Hemingway, Letter to family, November 1, 1918, Reprinted with the permission of Scribner, a division of Simon & Schuster LLC, from *The Letters of Ernest Hemingway: Volume 1 (1907–1922)*, edited by Sandra Spanier and Robert Trogdon Copyright © (New York: Cambridge University Press, 2011), 148–49. All rights reserved.

16. Agnes von Kurowsky to Ernest Hemingway, November 1, 1918, Hemingway Collection, John F. Kennedy Library, Boston, Massachusetts.

17. Agnes von Kurowsky to Ernest Hemingway, October 25, 1918, Hemingway Collection, John F. Kennedy Library, Boston, Massachusetts.

18. Agnes von Kurowsky to Ernest Hemingway, November 3, 1918, Hemingway Collection, John F. Kennedy Library, Boston, Massachusetts.

19. Agnes von Kurowsky to Ernest Hemingway, December 1, 1918, Hemingway Collection, John F. Kennedy Library, Boston, Massachusetts.

20. Agnes von Kurowsky to Ernest Hemingway, December 13, 1918, Hemingway Collection, John F. Kennedy Library, Boston, Massachusetts.

21. Agnes von Kurowsky to Ernest Hemingway, December 20, 1918, Hemingway Collection, John F. Kennedy Library, Boston, Massachusetts.

22. Agnes von Kurowsky to Ernest Hemingway, December 21, 1918, Hemingway Collection, John F. Kennedy Library, Boston, Massachusetts.

23. Ibid.

24. Bill Horne, quoted in Virginia Mosley, "Hemingway Remembered," *Barrington Courier-Review*, September 27, 1979, 28–33.

25. Agnes von Kurowsky to Ernest Hemingway, February 3, 1919, Hemingway Collection, John F. Kennedy Library, Boston, Massachusetts.

26. Agnes von Kurowsky to Ernest Hemingway, February 15, 1919, Hemingway Collection, John F. Kennedy Library, Boston, Massachusetts.

27. Ibid.

28. Agnes von Kurowsky to Ernest Hemingway, March 7, 1919, Ernest Hemingway Foundation of Oak Park Collection.

29. Ernest Hemingway to Bill Horne, March 30, 1919, Reprinted with the permission of Scribner, a division of Simon & Schuster LLC, from

The Letters of Ernest Hemingway: Volume 1 (1907–1922), edited by Sandra Spanier and Robert Trogdon Copyright © (New York: Cambridge University Press, 2011), 176–77. All rights reserved.

30. Ernest Hemingway to F. Scott Fitzgerld, May 28, 1934, from *The Letters of Ernest Hemingway: Volume 2 (1932–1934)*, edited by Sandra Spanier and Robert Trogdon (New York: Cambridge University Press, 2020), 614–16.

31. Ernest Hemingway, *A Farewell to Arms*, 16. Copyright © Hemingway Foreign Rights Trust. Reprinted with the permission of Scribner, a division of Simon & Schuster LLC. All rights reserved.

32. Ibid., 20.

33. Ibid., 55–56.

34. Ibid., 116.

35. Ibid. 92.

36. Idid., 114.

37. Ibid., 184–85.

38. Ibid., 184–85.

39. Ibid., 216.

40. Ibid., 224.

41. Ibid., 247.

42. Ibid.

43. Ibid.

44. Ibid., 251.

45. Ibid., 249.

46. Ibid., 327–28.

HADLEY

1. Marcelline Hemingway Sanford, *At the Hemingways* (Idaho: University of Idaho Press, 1999), 184.

2. Ibid., 189.

3. Ibid., 191.

4. Ibid.

5. Grace Hall Hemingway, Letter to Clarence Hemingway, July 28, 1920, quoted in James Nagel, *Ernest Hemingway: A Writer in Context* (Madison: University of Wisconsin Press, 1984), 81–82.

6. Grace Hall Hemingway, Letter to Ernest Hemingway, July 27, 1920, quoted in M. Reynolds, *Young Hemingway* (New York: Basel Blackwell, 1986), 137–38.

7. Ibid.

8. Ernest Hemingway, Letter to Howell Jenkins, September 16, 1920, Reprinted with permission of Simon & Schuster LLC from *The Letters of Ernest Hemingway: Volume 1 (1907–1922)*, edited by Sandra Spanier and Robert Trogdon. Copyright © (Cambridge University Press, 2011), 156–57. All rights reserved.

9. Hadley Richardson, Letter to Ernest Hemingway, November 8, 1920, Hemingway Collection, John F. Kennedy Library, Boston, Massachusetts.

10. Ernest Hemingway, quoted in Leister Hemingway, *My Brother Ernest Hemingway* (Cleveland: World, 1962), 71.

11. Hadley Richardson, Letter to Ernest Hemingway, December 27, 1920. Hemingway Collection, John F. Kennedy Library, Boston, Massachusetts.

12. Hadley Richardson, Letter to Ernest Hemingway, January 1, 1921. Hemingway Collection, John F. Kennedy Library, Boston, Massachusetts.

13. Hadley Richardson, quoted in Alice Sokoloff, *Hadley: The First Mrs. Hemingway* (New York: Dodd Mead, 1973), 21.

14. Ernest Hemingway, Letter to Grace Hall Hemingway, December 20, 1920, Reprinted with permission of Simon & Schuster LLC from *The Letters of Ernest Hemingway: Volume 1 (1907–1922)*, edited by Sandra Spanier and Robert Trogdon. Copyright © (Cambridge University Press, 2011), 255. All rights reserved.

15. Ernest Hemingway, Letter to Bill Smith, December 1920, Princeton University Library Collection.

16. Ibid.

17. Ernest Hemingway, Letter to Grace Hall Hemingway, Jan 1, 1921, Reprinted with permission of Simon & Schuster LLC from *The Letters of Ernest Hemingway: Volume 1 (1907–1922)*, edited by Sandra Spanier and Robert Trogdon. Copyright © (Cambridge University Press, 2011), 263–64. All rights reserved.

18. Hadley Richardson, Letter to Ernest Hemingway, November 11, 1920, Hemingway Collection, John F. Kennedy Library, Boston, Massachusetts.

19. Hadley Richardson, Letter to Ernest Hemingway, quoted in Sokoloff, *Hadley*, 22.

20. Hadley Richardson, Letter to Ernest Hemingway, quoted in Sokoloff, *Hadley*, 26–27.

21. Ibid.

22. Hadley Richardson, Letter to Ernest Hemingway, April 13, 1921, Princeton University Library Collection.

23. Ernest Hemingway, Letter to Bill Smith, April 28, 1921, Reprinted with permission of Simon & Schuster LLC from *The Letters of Ernest Hemingway: Volume 1 (1907–1922)*, edited by Sandra Spanier and Robert Trogdon. Copyright © (Cambridge University Press, 2011), 283. All rights reserved.

24. Hadley Richardson, Letter to Ernest Hemingway, August 21, 1921, Princeton University Library Collection.

25. Ernest Hemingway, Letter to family, Lilly Library, Indiana University, January 15, 1920, quoted in Michael Reynolds, *The Paris Years* (Cambridge, MA: Basil Blackwell, 1980), 17.

26. Ernest Hemingway, *A Moveable Feast*, 21, Copyright © Hemingway Foreign Rights Trust. Reprinted with the permission of Scribner, a division of Simon & Schuster LLC. All rights reserved. Reprinted by permission of Simon & Schuster (US) and The Random House Group Limited (UK).

27. Ibid., 22.

28. Ibid., 39.

29. Ibid., 53.

30. Marcelline Hemingway, *At the Hemingways*, 322.

31. Ibid.

32. Ernest Hemingway, "Three Day Blow," *The Complete Short Stories of Ernest Hemingway*, 90. Copyright © Hemingway Foreign Rights Trust. Reprinted with the permission of Scribner, a division of Simon & Schuster LLC. All rights reserved. Reprinted by permission of Simon & Schuster (US) and The Random House Group Limited (UK).

33. Ernest Hemingway, "Up in Michigan," *The Complete Short Stories of Ernest Hemingway*, 62. Copyright © Hemingway Foreign Rights Trust. Reprinted with the permission of Scribner, a division of Simon & Schuster LLC. All rights reserved. Reprinted by permission of Simon & Schuster (US) and The Random House Group Limited (UK).

34. Harold Loeb, quoted in Valerie Hemingway, *Running with the Bulls* (New York: Ballentine, 2005), 213.

35. Ernest Hemingway, *The Sun Also Rises*, 22. Copyright © Hemingway Foreign Rights Trust. Reprinted with the permission of Scribner, a division of Simon & Schuster LLC. All rights reserved. Reprinted by permission of Simon & Schuster (US) and The Random House Group Limited (UK).

36. Ibid., 144.

37. Ibid.

38. Ibid., 177.

39. Harold Loeb, quoted in Valerie Hemingway, *Running with the Bulls*, 213.

40. Pauline Pfeiffer, Letter to Hadley Richardson Hemingway, quoted in Bernice Kert, The *Hemingway Women* (New York: Norton, 1983), 176.

41. Ernest Hemingway, *A Moveable Feast*, 206, Copyright © Hemingway Foreign Rights Trust. Reprinted with the permission of Scribner, a division of Simon & Schuster LLC. All rights reserved. Reprinted by permission of Simon & Schuster (US) and The Random House Group Limited (UK).

42. Ernest Hemingway, quoted in Carlos Baker, *Ernest Hemingway: A Life Story* (New York: Scribner's, 1969), 164, 591.

43. Ernest Hemingway, *A Moveable Feast*, 206, Copyright © Hemingway Foreign Rights Trust. Reprinted with the permission of Scribner, a division of Simon & Schuster LLC. All rights reserved. Reprinted by permission of Simon & Schuster (US) and The Random House Group Limited (UK).

44. Ibid.

45. Ibid., 206–7.

46. Ibid., 207.

PAULINE

1. Ernest Hemingway, Letter to Ernest Walsh, January 2, 1926, *The Letters of Ernest Hemingway: Volume 2 (1926–1929)*, edited by Sandra Spanier and Robert Trogdon (Cambridge: Cambridge University Press, 2011), 6–7.

2. Matthew Nickel, "Young Hemingway's Wound and Conversion to Catholicism," *Pilgrim*, March 2013, 6.

3. Ernest Hemingway to A. E. Hotchner, *Hemingway and His World* (New York: Vendome Press, 1989), 108.

4. Ernest Hemingway, Letter to Guy Hickock, July 27, 1928, *The Letters of Ernest Hemingway: Volume 2 (1926–1929)*, edited by Sandra Spanier and Robert Trogdon (Cambridge: Cambridge University Press, 2011), 416–17.

5. Ernest Hemingway, Letter to Max Perkins, December 9, 1928, *The Letters of Ernest Hemingway: Volume 2 (1926–1929)*, edited by Sandra Spanier and Robert Trogdon (Cambridge: Cambridge University Press 2011), 479–80.

6. Ernest Hemingway, Letter to Grace Hall Hemingway, March 11, 1929, Reprinted with the permission of Scribner, a division of Simon & Schuster, from *Ernest Hemingway: Selected Letters 1917–1961*, Carlos Baker, editor, Copyright © 1981 by Carlos Baker and The Ernest Hemingway Foundation, Inc. All rights reserved. 295.

7. Leister Hemingway, *My Brother: Ernest Hemingway* (Cleveland: World, 1962), 109–10.

8. Grace Hall Hemingway to Ernest Hemingway, quoted in James R. Mellow, *Hemingway: A Life Without Consequences* (New York: Addison-Wesley Publishing, 1992), 390.

9. Ernest Hemingway, *Death in the Afternoon*, 122. Copyright © Hemingway Foreign Rights Trust. Reprinted with the permission of Scribner, a division of Simon & Schuster LLC. All rights reserved. Reprinted by permission of Simon & Schuster (US) and The Random House Group Limited (UK).

10. Ibid., 213.

11. Ibid., 103.

12. Pauline Hemingway, Letter to Ernest Hemingway, June 26, 1932, Princeton University Library Collection.

13. Ibid.

14. Ernest Hemingway, *The Green Hills of Africa*, Foreword. Copyright © Hemingway Foreign Rights Trust. Reprinted with the permission of Scribner, a division of Simon & Schuster LLC. All rights reserved. Reprinted by permission of Simon & Schuster (US) and The Random House Group Limited (UK).

15. Ibid., 21.

16. C. G. Poore, "Ernest Hemingway's Story of His African Safari," *New York Times*, October 27, 1935.

17. John Chamberlain, "Books of the Times," *New York Times*, October 25, 1935.

18. Jeffrey Meyers, *Hemingway: A Biography* (London: Macmillan, 1985), 252.

19. Ernest Hemingway, "The Short Happy Life of Francis Macomber," *The Complete Short Stories of Ernest Hemingway*, 17. Copyright © Hemingway Foreign Rights Trust. Reprinted with the permission of Scribner, a division of Simon & Schuster LLC. All rights reserved. Reprinted by permission of Simon & Schuster (US) and The Random House Group Limited (UK).

20. Ibid., 19.

21. Ibid., 9.

22. Ibid., 28.

23. Ibid., 9.

24. Ibid., 10.

25. Ibid., 18.

26. Ibid., 6.

27. Ernest Hemingway, "The Art of the Short Story," *Paris Review*, Spring 1981, 93.

28. Ernest Hemingway, "The Short Happy Life of Francis Macomber," *The Complete Short Stories of Ernest Hemingway*, 18. Copyright © Hemingway Foreign Rights Trust. Reprinted with the permission of Scribner, a division of Simon & Schuster LLC. All rights reserved. Reprinted by

permission of Simon & Schuster (US) and The Random House Group Limited (UK).

29. Ibid.

30. Ernest Hemingway, "The Art of the Short Story," 95.

31. Ernest Hemingway, "The Snows of Kilimanjaro," *The Complete Short Stories of Ernest Hemingway*, 43. Copyright © Hemingway Foreign Rights Trust. Reprinted with the permission of Scribner, a division of Simon & Schuster LLC. All rights reserved. Reprinted by permission of Simon & Schuster (US) and The Random House Group Limited (UK).

32. Ibid., 32.

33. Ibid., 49.

34. Ibid., 44.

35. Ibid., 43.

36. Ibid., 53.

37. Ernest Hemingway, *To Have and Have Not*, 28–31. Copyright © Hemingway Foreign Rights Trust. Reprinted by permission of Simon & Schuster (US) and The Random House Group Limited (UK).

38. Ibid., 240.

39. Ibid., 232.

40. Ibid., 150.

41. Ibid., 236.

42. Ibid., 225.

43. Meyers, *Hemingway*, 302.

MARTHA

1. Eleanor Roosevelt, quoted in Bernice Kert, *The Hemingway Women* (New York: Norton, 1983), 289.

2. Ernest Hemingway, *To Have and Have Not*, 238–39. Copyright © Hemingway Foreign Rights Trust. Reprinted with the permission of Scribner, a division of Simon & Schuster LLC. All rights reserved. Reprinted by permission of Simon & Schuster (US) and The Random House Group Limited (UK).

3. Ibid., 244–45.

4. Ibid.

5. Ernest Hemingway, Letter to the Pfeiffer family, February 9, 1937, Reprinted with the permission of Scribner, a division of Simon & Schuster LLC, from *Ernest Hemingway: Selected Letters, 1917–1961*, edited by Carlos Baker. Copyright © 1981 by Carlos Baker and the Ernest Hemingway Foundation, Inc. All rights reserved. 457.

6. Ernest Hemingway, Letter to Max Perkins, September 26, 1936, Reprinted with the permission of Scribner, a division of Simon & Schuster LLC, from *Ernest Hemingway: Selected Letters, 1917–1961*, edited by Carlos Baker, 454–55. Copyright © 1981 by Carlos Baker and the Ernest Hemingway Foundation, Inc. All rights reserved.

7. Charles Thompson, quoted in Kert, *The Hemingway Women*, 282.

8. Ernest Hemingway, "Mussolini, Europe's Prize Bluffer," in *Dateline Toronto*, edited by William White (New York: Charles Scribner's Sons, 1985), 253–59.

9. H. Matthews, quoted in John Raeburn, *Fame Became of Him: Hemingway as a Public Writer* (Bloomington IN: University Press, 1984), 87.

10. Martha Gellhorn, "Memory," *London Review of Books* 18, no. 24 (December 1996).

11. Ibid.

12. Ibid.

13. Ernest Hemingway to Stephen Spender, quoted in James R. Mellow, *Hemingway: A Life Without Consequences* (New York: Addison-Wesley Publishing, 1997), 504.

14. Ernest Hemingway, "Hemingway Reports Spain," *New Republic*, April 24, 1938, 350.

15. Martha Gellhorn, October 31, 1980, quoted in Kert, *The Hemingway Women*, 299.

16. Ernest Hemingway, "Shelling of Madrid," NANA Dispatch, April 11, 1937, in *By-Line: Ernest Hemingway*, edited by William White (New York: Charles Scribner's Sons, 1967), 259.

17. Ibid.

18. Ernest Hemingway, "Flight of the Refugees" NANA Dispatch, April 3, 1938, in *By-Line*, 281.

19. Ernest Hemingway, "The Barbarism of Fascist Interventionists in Spain," *Pravda*, August 1, 1938, reprinted in the *New York Times*, November 29, 1982.

20. Ibid.

21. Ibid.

22. Gellhorn, "Memory."

23. Ibid.

24. Ibid.

25. Ibid.

26. Ibid.

27. Martha Gellhorn to Eleanor Roosevelt, April 24, 1938, quoted in Kert, *The Hemingway Women*, 321.

28. Ibid., 316.

29. Ernest Hemingway, "The Barbarism of Fascist Interventionists in Spain."

30. Ernest Hemingway, *For Whom the Bell Tolls*, 22. Copyright © Hemingway Foreign Rights Trust. Reprinted with the permission of Scribner, a division of Simon & Schuster LLC. All rights reserved. Reprinted by permission of Simon & Schuster (US) and The Random House Group Limited (UK).

31. Ibid., 235.

32. Ibid., 467.

33. Ibid., 236.

34. John Donne, "Mediations VII," quoted in Hemingway, *For Whom the Bell Tolls* (New York, Scribner and Sons, 1940).

35. Martha Gellhorn, quoted in Kert, *The Hemingway Women*, 348.

36. Ernest Hemingway, Letter to Carol Hemingway, 1945, quoted in Norberto Fuentes, *Hemingway in Cuba* (Secaucus, NJ: Lyle Stuart, 1984), 387–88.

37. Martha Gellhorn to Edna Gellhorn, quoted in Kert, *The Hemingway Women*, 354.

38. Ernest Hemingway to Max Perkins, August 27, 1942, Reprinted with the permission of Scribner, a division of Simon & Schuster LLC, from *Ernest Hemingway: Selected Letters, 1917–1961*, edited by Carlos

Baker, 541. Copyright © 1981 by Carlos Baker and the Ernest Hemingway Foundation, Inc. All rights reserved.

39. Ernest Hemingway to Martha Gellhorn Hemingway, Telegram, quoted in Kert, *The Hemingway Women*, 391.

40. Martha Gellhorn Hemingway to Ernest Hemingway, June 26, 1943, quoted in Kert, *The Hemingway Women*, 379.

41. Ibid.

42. Hemingway FBI file, R. Gordon Leddy to J. Edgar Hoover, October 8, 1942.

43. Hemingway FBI file, R. Gordon Leddy to C. H. Carson, October 9, 1942.

44. Kert, *The Hemingway Women*, 302.

45. Ernest Hemingway, Letter to Patrick Hemingway, November 19, 1944, Reprinted with the permission of Scribner, a division of Simon & Schuster LLC, from *Ernest Hemingway: Selected Letters, 1917–1961*, edited by Carlos Baker, 576. Copyright © 1981 by Carlos Baker and the Ernest Hemingway Foundation, Inc. All rights reserved.

46. Hemingway FBI file, R. Gordon Leddy to J. Edgar Hoover, June 26, 1943.

47. Ernest Hemingway, quoted in Gregory Hemingway, *Papa* (New York: Houghton Mifflin, 1976), 91–92.

48. Matha Gellhorn, Letter to Ernest Hemingway, December 12, 1943, quoted in Kert, *The Hemingway Women*, 388.

49. Ernest Hemingway, Letter to Martha Gellhorn, January 31, 1944, Hemingway Collection, John F. Kennedy Library and Presidential Museum.

50. Spruille Braden to Ernest Hemingway, March 7, 1944, quoted in a letter to Charles Colepaugh March 30, 1944, Hemingway Collection, John F. Kennedy Library and Presidential Museum.

51. Martha Gellhorn, February 15, 1982, quoted in Kert, *The Hemingway Women*, 392.

52. Ibid.

53. Ernest Hemingway "Voyage to Victory," *Collier's*, July 22, 1944, in *By-Line*, 355.

54. Harold Acton, *Memoirs of an Aesthete* (New York: Viking, 1970).

55. Martha Gellhorn, February 15, 1982, quoted in Kert, *The Hemingway Women*, 417.

MARY

1. Letter from David Bruce, 1947–1948, Hemingway Collection John F. Kennedy Library, Boston, quoted in A. E. Hotchner, *Hemingway and His World* (New York: Vendome Press, 1989), 160.

2. Ernest Hemingway to Mary Welsh Monks, quoted in Mary Welsh Hemingway, *How It Was* (New York: Knopf, 1976), 93–94.

3. Ibid.

4. Ibid.

5. Ibid.

6. Bill Walton, Letter to B. Kert, April 1980, quoted in Bernice Kert, *The Hemingway Women* (New York: Norton, 1983), 403.

7. Kert, *The Hemingway Women*, 409.

8. Ernest Hemingway, Letter to Mary Welsh, quoted in Norberto Fuentes, *Hemingway in Cuba* (Secaucus, NJ: Lyle Stuart, 1984), 353.

9. Ernest Hemingway, Letter to Patrick Hemingway, November 19, 1944, Reprinted with the permission of Scribner, a division of Simon & Schuster LLC, from *Ernest Hemingway: Selected Letters 1917–1961*, edited by Carlos Baker, 576. Copyright © 1981 by Carlos Baker and The Ernest Hemingway Foundation, Inc. All rights reserved.

10. Ernest Hemingway to Pauline Hemingway, quoted in Mary Welsh Hemingway, *How It Was*, 133.

11. Ibid., 153.

12. Ibid., 156.

13. Ernest Hemingway, *Look*, 1956, quoted in Hotchner, *Hemingway and His World*, 167.

14. Irwin Shaw, *The Young Lions* (New York: Modern Library, 1948), 382.

15. Ibid.

16. Mary Welsh Hemingway, *How It Was*, 323.

17. Ernest Hemingway, *Across the River and Into the Trees.*, 282. Copyright © Hemingway Foreign Rights Trust. Reprinted with the permission of Scribner, a division of Simon & Schuster LLC. All rights

reserved. Reprinted by permission of Simon & Schuster (US) and The Random House Group Limited (UK).

18. Ibid., 233.

19. Ibid., 235.

20. Ibid., 195.

21. Ibid., 197.

22. Ibid., 78–79.

23. Ibid., 145.

24. Ibid.

25. Adriana Ivancich, Letter to Berice Kert, October 1980, quoted in Kert, *The Hemingway Women*, 450.

26. Ibid.

27. Ibid.

28. Ibid., 443.

29. Ibid., 456.

30. Mary Welsh Hemingway, *How It Was*, 283.

31. M. Geismar, *Saturday Review of Literature*, quoted in James R. Mellow, *Hemingway: A Life Without Consequences* (New York: Addison-Wesley Publishing, 1992), 560.

32. J. Donald Adams, "Speaking of Books," *New York Times*, September 24, 1950.

33. Ernest Hemingway, quoted in Mellow, *Hemingway*, 559.

34. Ernest Hemingway, *Conversations with Ernest Hemingway*, edited by M. Brucoli (Jackson, MS: University Press of Mississippi, 1986), 61–62.

35. Ernest Hemingway, quoted in Mellow, *Hemingway*, 561.

36. Ernest Hemingway, quoted in Carlos Baker, "Introduction," *Hemingway and His Critics* (New York: Hill and Wang, 1961), 10.

37. Ernest Hemingway, *The Old Man and the Sea*, 103, Copyright © Hemingway Foreign Rights Trust, Reprinted with the permission of Scribner, a division of Simon & Schuster LLC. All rights reserved. Reprinted by permission of Simon & Schuster (US) and The Random House Group Limited (UK).

38. Ernest Hemingway, quoted in Mary Welsh Hemingway, *How It Was*, 286.

39. Ibid.

40. Ernest Hemingway, *The Old Man and the Sea*, 127. Copyright © Hemingway Foreign Rights Trust. Reprinted with the permission of Scribner, a division of Simon & Schuster LLC. All rights reserved.

41. Mark Schorer, "The New Republic," quoted in Mellow, *Hemingway*, 581.

42. Orville Prescott, "New York Times," quoted in Mellow, *Hemingway*, 581.

43. Kert, *The Hemingway Women*, 471.

44. Ibid.

45. Ibid., 472.

46. Ernest Hemingway, "Ernest Hemingway: Banquet Speech," https://www.nobelprize.org/prizes/literature/1954/hemingway/speech/.

47. Ernest Hemingway to Patrick Hemingway, November 24, 1958, Reprinted with the permission of Scribner, a division of Simon & Schuster LLC, from *Ernest Hemingway: Selected Letters 1917–1961*, edited by Carlos Baker, 887–88. Copyright © 1981 by Carlos Baker and The Ernest Hemingway Foundation, Inc. All rights reserved.

48. Ernest Hemingway, Letter to Mary Welsh Hemingway, August 1960, in Mary Welsh Hemingway, *How It Was*, 489.

49. Mary Welsh Hemingway, quoted in Hotchner, *Hemingway and His World*, 200.

50. Ibid.

51. Ernest Hemingway, quoted in M. Reynolds, *Hemingway: The Final Years* (New York: Norton, 1999), 335.

52. Ernest Hemingway, Letter to L. H. Brague, Januray 24, 1959, Reprinted with the permission of Scribner, a division of Simon & Schuster LLC, from *Erneset Hemingway: Selected Letters 1917–1961*, edited by Carlos Baker, 892. Copyright © 1981 by Carlos Baker and The Ernest Hemingway Foundation, Inc. All rights reserved.

53. Ernest Hemingway, quoted in Mary Welsh Hemingway, *How It Was*, 568.

54. Mary Welsh Hemingway, *How It Was*, 500–2.

EPILOGUE

1. Ernest Hemingway to George Plimpton, "An Interview with Ernest Hemingway," in *Hemingway and His Critics*, edited by Carlos Baker (New York: Hill and Wang, 1961).

2. Bill Horne, quoted in Virginia Moseley, "Hemingway Remembered," *Barrington Courier-Review*, September 27, 1979, 28–33.

3. Leicester Hemingway, *My Brother: Ernest Hemingway* (Cleveland: World, 1962), 14–16.

4. Ernest Hemingway, quoted in Mary Welsh Hemingway, *How It Was* (New York: Alfred A. Knopf, 1976), 504.

5. Quentin Reynolds to J. Edgar Hoover, letter dated January 6, 1964, contained in Hemingway Federal Bureau of Investigation file.

6. Ibid.

7. Martha Gellhorn, quoted in Rick Lyman, "Martha Gellhorn, Daring Writer, Dies at 89," *New York Times*, February 17, 1998. https://www.nytimes.com/1998/02/17/arts/martha-gellhorn-daring-writer-dies-at-89.html.

8. Martha Gellhorn, quoted in "I Didn't Like Sex at All," *Salon*, August 12, 2006.

9. Martha Gellhorn, quoted in Lyman, "Martha Gellhorn, Daring Writer, Dies at 89."

10. Jack Hemingway, quoted in Lyman, "Martha Gellhorn, Daring Writer, Dies at 89."

11. Ernest Hemingway, quoted in Bernice Kert, *The Hemingway Women* (New York: W.W. Norton, 1983), 344.

12. Hadley Richardson Hemingway, quoted in Kert, *The Hemingway Women*, 189.

13. Ibid., 199.

14. Ibid., 205.

15. Ernest Hemingway, Letter to Hadley Mowrer, January 1938, Reprinted with the permission of Scribner, a division of Simon & Schuster LLC, from *Ernest Hemingway: Selected Letters 1917–1961*, edited by Carlos Baker, 463. Copyright © 1981 by Carlos Baker and The Ernest Hemingway Foundation, Inc. All rights reserved.

16. Ernest Hemingway, Letter to F. Scott Fitzgerald, July 1, 1925, Reprinted with the permission of Scribner, a division of Simon & Schuster LLC, from *Ernest Hemingway: Selected Letters 1917–1961*, edited by Carlos Baker, 165–66. Copyright © 1981 by Carlos Baker and The Ernest Hemingway Foundation, Inc. All rights reserved.

17. Oak Park River Forest High School yearbook, 1917, quoted in N. Sindelar, *Influencing Hemingway* (Landham, MD: Rowman & Littlefield, 2014), 23.

18. Marlene Dietrich, "The Most Fascinating Man I Know," *New York Herald Tribune*, February 13, 1955, 8–9.

19. Ibid.

20. Ibid.

21. Ibid.

22. Ibid.

23. Ernest Hemingway to Marlene Dietrich, July 1, 1950, Hemingway Collection, John F. Kennedy Presidential Library, Boston.

24. Ibid.

BIBLIOGRAPHY

Acton, Harold. *Memoir of an Aesthete*. New York: Viking, 1970.

Adams, J. Donald. "Speaking of Books." *New York Times*, September 24, 1950.

Baker, Carlos. *Ernest Hemingway: A Life Story*. New York: Charles Scribner's Sons, 1969.

Baker, Carlos, ed. *Hemingway and His Critics*. New York: Hill and Wang, 1961.

Baker, Sheridan. *Ernest Hemingway: An Introduction and Interpretation*. Ann Arbor, MI: University of Michigan, 1967.

Biggs, Fannie. *Memories of Ernest Hemingway*. Charles Fenton Papers, February 24, 1952. Yale Collection of American Literature, Beinecke Rare Book Room and Manuscript Collection, Yale University.

Braden, Spruille. *Diplomats and Demagogues*. New York: Arlington House, 1971.

Chamberlain, John. "Books of the Times." *New York Times*, October 25, 1935.

Dietrich, Marlene. "The Most Fascinating Man I Know." *New York Herald Tribune*, February 1955, 8–9.

Donnelly, Honoria, and Richard Billings. *Sara & Gerald*. New York: Times Books, 1982.

Fuentes, Norberto. *Hemingway in Cuba*. Secaucus, NJ: Lyle Stuart, 1984.

Gellhorn, Martha. "I Didn't Like Sex at All." *Salon*, August 12, 2006.

———. "Memory." *London Review of Books* 18, no. 24 (December 1996).

Griffin, Peter. *Along with Youth*. New York: Oxford University Press, 1985.

Hemingway, Anson. *Civil War Journal*. May 1863, Special Collections, Oak Park Public Library, Oak Park, Illinois.

Hemingway, Clarence. Letter to Ernest Hemingway, July 17, 1918. Hemingway Collection. John F. Kennedy Library, Boston.

Hemingway, Ernest. *Across the River and Into the Trees*. Copyright © Hemingway Foreign Rights Trust. Reprinted with the permission of Scribner, a division of Simon & Schuster LLC. All rights reserved. Reprinted by permission of Simon & Schuster (US) and The Random House Group Limited (UK).

———. "The Art of the Short Story." *The Paris Review* (spring 1981).

———. "The Barbarism of Fascist Interventionists in Spain." *Pravda*, August 1, 1938. Reprinted in the *New York Times*, November 29, 1982.

———. *By-Line: Ernest Hemingway*, edited by W. White. New York: Charles Scribner's Sons, 1967.

———. *The Complete Short Stories of Ernest Hemingway*. New York: Charles Scribner's Sons, 1987. Copyright © Hemingway Foreign Rights Trust. Reprinted with the permission of Scribner, a division of Simon & Schuster LLC. All rights reserved. Reprinted by permission of Simon & Schuster (US) and The Random House Group Limited (UK).

———. *Conversations with Ernest Hemingway*, edited by Matthew Bruccoli. Jackson, MS: University Press of Mississippi, 1986.

———. *Dateline Toronto*, edited by W. White. New York: Charles Scribner's Sons, 1985.

———. *Death in the Afternoon*. Copyright © Hemingway Foreign Rights Trust. Reprinted with the permission of Scribner, a division of Simon & Schuster LLC. All rights reserved. Reprinted by permission of Simon & Schuster (US) and The Random House Group Limited (UK).

———. *Ernest Hemingway: Selected Letters 1917–1961*, edited by Carlos Baker. Copyright © 1981 by Carlos Baker and The Ernest Hemingway Foundation, Inc. Reprinted with the permission of Scribner, a division of Simon & Schuster LLC. All rights reserved.

———. *A Farewell to Arms*. Copyright © Hemingway Foreign Rights Trust. Reprinted with the permission of Scribner, a division of Simon & Schuster LLC. All rights reserved. Reprinted by

permission of Simon & Schuster (US) and The Random House Group Limited (UK).

——. *For Whom the Bell Tolls*. Copyright © Hemingway Foreign Rights Trust. Reprinted with the permission of Scribner, a division of Simon & Schuster LLC. All rights reserved. Reprinted by permission of Simon & Schuster (US) and The Random House Group Limited (UK).

——. *The Green Hills of Africa*. Copyright © Hemingway Foreign Rights Trust. Reprinted with the permission of Scribner, a division of Simon & Schuster LLC. All rights reserved. Reprinted by permission of Simon & Schuster (US) and The Random House Group Limited (UK).

——. "Hemingway Reports Spain." *The New Republic* 94 (April 24, 1938).

——. Letter to Bill Horne, March 13, 1919 Ernest Hemingway Foundation of Oak Park Collection.

——. *The Letters of Ernest Hemingway: Volume 1 (1907–1922)*, edited by Sandra Spanier and Robert Trogdon. Copyright © (Cambridge University Press, 2011). Reprinted with permission of Simon & Schuster LLC.

——. *The Letters of Ernest Hemingway: Volume 2. (1926–1929)*, edited by Sandra Spanier and Robert Trogdon. New York: Cambridge University Press, 2011.

——. *A Moveable Feast*. Copyright © Hemingway Foreign Rights Trust. Reprinted with the permission of Scribner, a division of Simon & Schuster LLC. All rights reserved. Reprinted by permission of Simon & Schuster (US) and The Random House Group Limited (UK).

——. "Nobel Prize Banquet Speech." https://www.nobelprize.org/prizes/literature/1954/hemingway/speech/. Manuscript Collection, Yale University.

——. *The Old Man and the Sea*. Copyright © Hemingway Foreign Rights Trust. Reprinted with the permission of Scribner, a division of Simon & Schuster LLC. All rights reserved. Reprinted by

permission of Simon & Schuster (US) and The Random House Group Limited (UK).

———. *The Sun Also Rises.* Copyright © Hemingway Foreign Rights Trust. Reprinted with the permission of Scribner, a division of Simon & Schuster LLC. All rights reserved. Reprinted by permission of Simon & Schuster (US) and The Random House Group Limited (UK).

———. *Three Stories and Ten Poems.* Paris: Contact Publishing, 1923.

———. *To Have and Have Not.* Copyright © Hemingway Foreign Rights Trust. Reprinted with the permission of Scribner, a division of Simon & Schuster LLC. All rights reserved. Reprinted by permission of Simon & Schuster (US) and The Random House Group Limited (UK).

———. *The Trapeze.* Oak Park, Illinois: Oak Park and River Forest High School, 1916.

Hemingway, Grace Hall. Letter to Ernest Hemingway, April 17, 1918. Hemingway Collection, John F. Kennedy Library, Boston.

———. *Memory Book I and II.* Hemingway Collection, John F. Kennedy Presidential Library, Boston.

Hemingway, Gregory. *Papa.* New York: Houghton Mifflin, 1976.

Hemingway, Leicester. *My Brother: Ernest Hemingway.* Cleveland: World, 1962.

Hemingway, Mary Welsh. *How It Was.* New York: Alfred A. Knopf, 1976.

Hemingway, Pauline Pfieffer. Pauline Pfieffer Hemingway Collection, Princeton University Library, Princeton, New Jersey.

Hemingway, Valerie. *Running with the Bulls.* New York: Ballentine, 2005.

Hotchner, A. E. *Hemingway and His World.* New York: Vendome Press, 1989.

Kert, Bernice. *The Hemingway Women.* New York: W.W. Norton, 1983.

Leddy, R. Gordon. Letters to J. Edgar Hoover and C.H. Carson, October 8 and 9, 1942. https://vault.fbi.gov/ernest-miller-hemingway/ernest-hemingway-part-01-of-01/.

Lewis, Robert. "Hemingway in Italy." *Journal of Modern Literature* (May 1982): 215.

Lyman, Rick. "Martha Gellhorn, Daring Writer, Dies at 89." *New York Times*, February 17, 1998. https://www.nytimes.com/1998/02/17/arts/martha-gellhorn-daring-writer-dies-at-89.html.

Lynn, Kenneth. *Hemingway*. New York: Simon and Schuster, 1987.

Mellow, J. *Hemingway: A Life Without Consequences*. New York: Addison Wesley, 1992.

Meyers, Jeffery. *Hemingway*. New York: Harper Rowe, 1985.

Mosley, Virginia. "Hemingway Remembered." *Barrington Courier-Review*, September 27, 1979, 28–33.

Nagel, James. *Ernest Hemingway: A Writer in Context*. Madison: University of Wisconsin Press, 1984.

Nickel, Matthew. "Young Hemingway's Wound and Conversion to Catholicism." *Pilgrim* (March 2013): 1–13.

Poore, C. G. "Ernest Hemingway's Story of His African Safari." *New York Times*, October 27, 1935.

Raeburn, John. *Fame Became of Him: Hemingway as a Public Writer*. Bloomington, IN: University Press, 1984.

Reynolds, Michael. *The Paris Years*. Cambridge, MA: Basil Blackwell, 1980.

———. *The Final Years*. New York: Norton, 1999.

———. *Young Hemingway*. New York: Basel Blackwell, 1986.

Reynolds, Quentin, to J. Edgar Hoover. January 6, 1964. https://vault.fbi.gov/ernest-miller-hemingway/ernest-hemingway-part-01-of-01/.

Richardson, Hadley. The Hadley Richardson Letters Collection, John F. Kennedy Presidential Library, Boston. Princeton University Library Collection, Princeton, New Jersey.

Sanford, Marcelline. *At the Hemingways*. Moscow, ID: University of Idaho Press, 1999.

Shaw, Irwin. *The Young Lions*. New York: Modern Library, 1948.

Sindelar, Nancy. *Influencing Hemingway*. Lanham, MD: Rowman & Littlefield, 2014.

Sokoloff, Alice. *Hadley: The First Mrs. Hemingway*. New York: Dodd Mead, 1973.

Whiting, Charles. *Hemingway Goes to War*. Gloucestershire, England: Sutton, 1999.

Villard, H., and J. Nagel. *Hemingway in Love and War: The Lost Diary of Agnes Von Kurkowsky*. Boston: Northeastern University Press, 1989.

Von Kurowsky, Agnes. Letter to Ernest Hemingway, March 7, 1919. Ernest Hemingway Foundation of Oak Park Collection.

————. The Agnes Von Kurowsky Letters Collection, John F. Kennedy Presidential Library, Boston.

Index

in, 106, 135; Mary in, 139–40,
141, 150, 163, 198; Paris memoirs, 96–97, 159; Pauline in,
70, 73, 78, 79, *80–81*, 98, 106,
190, 195
The Paris Wife (McLain), 180
Pauline. *See* Pfeiffer, Pauline
Percival, Philip, 91, 158
periodicals: *Chicago Daily News*,
178; *Cleveland Star*, 78;
Collier's, 134–35, 141, 172, 196;
Cooperative Commonwealth,
57–58, 194; *Duetsche Zentral
Zeitung, 113*; *Esquire*, 88, 91,
185; *Kansas City Star*, 15, 22,
108, 193; *Ken*, 117; *Life*, 163,
198; *PM*, 124–26; *Pravda*, 116,
118; *Tabula*, 16; *Toronto Star*,
14, 47, 53, 59, 64, 65, 194;
Transatlantic Review, 65, 67,
194; *Trapeze*, 15–16; *Vanity
Fair*, 78
Perkins, Max, 73, 82, 83–84, 106,
127, 128, 175
Pfeiffer, Gus (Uncle Gus), 78,
82, 84, 88, *89*, 91, 98, 99, 100,
104, 174
Pfeiffer, Pauline, *77*, *87*, 105,
106, 151, *176*, 185, 193; affair
with Ernest, 73–74, 76, 177,
178; in Africa, 91, 98, 158,
175, 195; birth of son Patrick,
49, 82; death of, 177, 197;
divorce from Ernest, 122, 173,
175, 196; *To Have and Have

Not, fictionalized in, 100,
104; in Key West, 79–80, 81,
85, 88–90, 98, 143, 175, 195;
marriage to Ernest, 79, *80*,
178, 195; in Paris, 70, 73, 78,
79, *80–81*, 98, 106, 190, 195;
in Spain, 67, 70, *72*, 78, 84,
100, 156, 177, 1946, 195; as
wealthy, 70, 76, 83, 93–94, 95,
96, 100, 174
Pilar cabin cruiser, 85, *131*, 132,
133, 144, *153*, 155, 165, 170,
188, 195, 196
Pivano, Fernanda, 47
Platt, Frank, 38
Poore, C. G., 93
Pound, Ezra, 24, 59, 63, 65, 67, 74

Regler, Gustav, 112, *113*
Reynolds, Quentin, 170–71
Rice, Alfred, 168
Richardson, Hadley (Mowrer), *51*,
106, 141, 151, 175, *179*, 190,
193; in Austria, *68*, 73, *75*, 76,
78; Bryn Mawr, attending, 55,
106; courtship and wedding
to Ernest, 55–58, *60–61*, 194;
death of, 1802, 198; divorce
from Ernest, 74, 79, 178–79,
195; frugal lifestyle, 64–65, 83,
98; *A Moveable Feast,* fictionalized in, 64–65, 74, 177, 181;
pain of leaving, Ernest experiencing, 84, 85; in Paris, 59,
62, 63–67, 73–74, 98, 177, 180,

About the Author

Nancy W. Sindelar has spent more than thirty years in education as a teacher, administrator, university professor, and consultant and has published numerous articles and three books on educational topics. Her interest in Hemingway was nurtured as she taught American literature at Oak Park and River Forest High School, Hemingway's alma mater, and as a thirty-two-year resident of Oak Park River Forest, Hemingway's home from birth until his departure to Kansas City after graduation from high school.

Nancy is the author of *Influencing Hemingway: The People and Places That Shaped His Life and Work* and a popular presenter on the life and work of Ernest Hemingway. She has made multiple presentations at the International Colloquium Ernest Hemingway in Havana, Cuba; the American Literature Association Conferences in Washington, DC, Boston, and San Francisco; the Hemingway Society Conferences in Venice, Italy and Oak Park, Illinois, Paris, France, Sheridan, Wyoming, and San Sebastian, Spain; and keynoted the Hemingway Festivals in Sun Valley, Idaho. She also has presented at the American Library in Paris, keynoted the Michigan Hemingway Society Conference and the Hemingway Days Festival in Key West, Florida, and guided walking tours through young Hemingway's Oak Park.

Interested in working with private organizations, book clubs, and groups wanting to learn more about the life of Ernest Hemingway, she has been a guest lecturer at numerous libraries and universities, a cultural enrichment speaker on luxury cruises to Cuba and the Caribbean, and lived in Hemingway's Ketchum, Idaho home as the 2021 Writer-in-Residence. Her presentations are energized by her passion for all things Hemingway, her research into his private letters, his fiction and nonfiction, and her extensive travel to and knowledge of the locales that were important to the writer. She has stood in the bedroom where Hemingway was born and the foyer where he ended his life and has visited all the places in between.

Nancy is a board member of the Ernest Hemingway Foundation of Oak Park and teaches Hemingway: The Man, The Writer, The Legend at University of California, Riverside. She holds a BS in English, MA in literature, CAS in educational administration, and a PhD in educational leadership and policy studies.